Silf, Margaret.

Compass points.

DATE			

Other books by Margaret Silf

Inner Compass: An Invitation to Ignatian Spirituality

Close to the Heart: A Guide to Personal Prayer

Going on Retreat: A Beginner's Guide to the Christian Retreat Experience

COMPASS

MEETING GOD EVERY DAY AT EVERY TURN

POINTS

MARGARET SILF

LOYOLAPRESS.
A JESUIT MINISTRY
Chicago

LOYOLA PRESS.
A JESUIT MINISTRY

3441 N. Ashland Avenue
Chicago, Illinois 60657
(800) 621-1008
www.loyolapress.com

Cover image by Johner/Johner Images/Getty Images
Cover design by Judine O'Shea
Interior design by Maggie Hong

Library of Congress Cataloging-in-Publication Data
Silf, Margaret.
Compass points / Margaret Silf.
p. cm.
ISBN-13: 978-0-8294-2810-0
ISBN-10: 0-8294-2810-0
1. Meditations. I. Title.
BV4832.3.S54 2009
242—dc22

2008050681

Printed in the United States of America
09 10 11 12 13 14 Versa 10 9 8 7 6 5 4 3 2 1

For Alexa Storm,
newly arrived in this world.

May wisdom guide your journey,
and may love accompany your every step.

Contents

Introduction

God has escaped from the sanctuary.

Is that bad news or good news? For some people it might be a terrifying thought, because if God isn't confined to our holy places, how will we know where to find God? Will we ever be able to find God at all? For others it is a liberating thought, because if God gets loose, then God is potentially to be found *everywhere,* including, of course, the sanctuary.

God is in all things—this is a well-known observation. It's the kind of thing we say without really knowing what we mean. It's the kind of thing we wish we could really believe. If God is indeed in all things, then why does God often seem to be so elusive? Why do we so often have to ask, "Where is God in all of this?"

Compass Points is written out of the conviction that God isn't as elusive as we think, and certainly isn't stuck in a holy box that we visit only on Sundays. Like the light shining through the image on the cover, the God who runs through *Compass Points* is likely to turn up just about anywhere—on a boardwalk, in the movement of water, in the energy and curiosity of a child, and in the sparkling presence that flickers through a fountain. God is in the big story of our human journey on planet earth, in our origins and in our destiny and in every moment in between. And God is in all the smaller but equally amazing stories of how our individual lives move on, step by step and day by day. God is in the light and in the shadows of our experience, in what we rejoice in and in what we grieve over. God is both the dream we follow and the inspiration for our quest. God is in every choice we make, always urging us, prompting us, and coaxing us to choose life. When our lives fall apart, God is right there, waiting and longing to lead us beyond breakdown to breakthrough.

The first time I held Alexa Storm, to whom this book is dedicated, she was only a few minutes old. I felt closer to her than to my own next breath, and yet I knew I was also gazing upon a new human life packed with mystery. The same paradox is present in our sense of the divine. God is in the everyday details of everything we are and do, feel and think, and yet God remains and will always remain utterly mysterious. And, like Alexa, God evokes a personal response from us. A child calls forth our deepest desire to nurture and guide and love. God calls forth our deepest desire, not just to strive to know God better, but to seek to love each other with the kind of love God reveals.

As we journey we will travel through all the points of the compass, reminding ourselves that God is waiting to meet us in every possible direction. Yet in all our journeying what matters most is not where we are *going*, but how we are *being*, here and now in this present moment. God is ever-*present*—not, as we may have grown up believing, either ever-past or ever-future. The ever-present is a dynamic reality that can't be boxed in or defined, but can only be experienced. *Compass Points* pauses in every direction, catches snapshots of God's footprints, and invites you simply to "look *here*," wherever you happen to be and however you are feeling.

The reflections in this book are very personal and are gathered from my own daily journeying. *Your* encounters with the living God are your own. They will be different. They will be unique. Don't follow my footprints, but make your own. And maybe share them too, with trusted friends, because God encounters multiply when they are shared, like seeds falling on fertile ground. My only desire in sharing some glimpses of my daily journeying is to encourage you to seek God in your own, and perhaps to help you recognize and respond to the divine present-ness wherever you meet it.

Readers who are familiar with the spirituality of St. Ignatius Loyola will readily recognize the debt this book and its author owe to the Ignatian tradition. The journey round the compass points reflects the most important themes of the Spiritual Exercises. However, this dynamic is not confined to any one approach to the spiritual journey. It is powerful precisely because it reflects the dynamic of most people's search for God, whatever their spiritual background. *Compass Points* is a brief excursion to show how reflective prayer on our daily experience might look in practice. Keep in mind, however, that there are as many ways of praying as there are people trying to pray. Let your own ways suggest themselves, and trust them to lead you into your unique pathways with God.

Thank you for joining me in this adventure of awareness that doesn't ask you to make long journeys, read erudite books, or attend expensive programs, but simply to be present to the life you are actually living, and to discover for yourself the myriad ways in which the light of God shines through your minutes and your days.

MARGARET SILF

NANTWICH, ENGLAND, AUGUST 2008

NORTH

Origins

Where do I come from? The question is as old as humanity and as new as every inquiring child. The longing to discover our deepest roots stirs in every human heart. We want to know who gave us birth. We want to know the name of the soil in which we were first planted. To know where we come from is another way of exploring who we really are. It is also a way of saying that we know we are not islands in this great ocean of being we call life. We know that we are all interconnected, part of a continuum, single strands in a mighty tapestry.

We begin our journey here at North, our origins, and we will end it by returning to North, our destiny. But the journey will change us, and when we come full circle we shall know ourselves anew. As we saunter through our earliest beginnings, we meet ourselves, each other, and God, in the depths of the canyons, in the vast expanse of the stars, in the Australian deserts and the African plains, on mountain tops and in rushing rivers. And we awaken to the startled awareness that all we are, and ever shall be, is also mirrored in the minutiae of every day—in the ultrasound scan, in the vegetable plot, and even in the car wash.

Welcome to who you are. Let God introduce you to God's best-kept secret.

The Baobab Tree | 1

I HAVE A BAOBAB TREE, OR AT LEAST A HANDCRAFTED representation of one, which I brought back from South Africa. The importance of the baobab first caught my attention when I watched a television documentary filmed in Tanzania. In a remote rural village stood an ancient baobab, already completely hollowed out by the passing of the centuries. Its roots reached deep into the African earth. Its branches stretched out to the brilliant blue skies and the star-laden canopy that have captured the human imagination since *Homo sapiens* took their first bipedal steps here and told their stories around the campfire in the equatorial night.

This was a sacred tree, not only because of its ancient lineage, but also because it was the community's birthing tree. Whenever a pregnant woman came to her term, she would enter into the hollowed-out sanctuary of the baobab, give birth to her child, and remain there with her young until the umbilical cord fell away. Every child in the village had first seen the light of day within the enfolding shelter of that tree. It had literally borne the fruit of the human family in that place, delighting them with its large white flowers and nourishing them with its gourdlike fruit.

My own baobab sits in a very different rural community, in the heart of the English countryside. Yet, because I know something of its history, it takes me back, every day, to a place of origin, deeper than the soil of our planet and deeper than human memory—a space before and beyond space-time, where all is One, and the One is birthed within the arms of God.

Weathered into Glory | 2

BRYCE CANYON, IN UTAH, IS MAGICAL IN THE predawn hours, when the light of the just-rising sun sets the rock columns alight, as if with an inner fire.

You could almost imagine that this inner fire is the living afterglow of that first flaring forth of our universe, billions of years ago. The hoodoos are so amazingly beautiful, not because they have acquired layers of grandeur through the millennia, but because they have *lost* so much. Their beauty is revealed because they have suffered aeons of erosion, as the biting winds and the flash floods stripped them down to their essential core. When you go down to the depths of the canyon at dawn, you can meet the Creator at work and tune in to this great paradox: creation and destruction are the yin and yang of the one life-generating power we call God.

Could it be that our personal diminishments might also, sometimes, reveal a deeper beauty we never guessed was there? I reflect on a few people I have known, whose lives seem to illustrate the truth of this proposition. At the nadir of their lives—perhaps in terminal illness, or in the throes of some tragic event—they have seemed to be shining with an inner light that has illumined the lives of those around them.

A story is told of a young girl who had a good singing voice. Her parents didn't want to put her through the stress of professional musical training unless they were assured that she had a special talent, so they asked a musician friend to give her an informal audition in their home. When she had sung for him, he sat back and considered his verdict. "She sings beautifully," he said at last. "When her heart has been broken she will sing sublimely."

The hoodoos tell the same story. These pinnacles were always beautiful. But after having suffered the lashings of wind and water for countless millennia, they have indeed become sublime. Locked up in every rock is a work of breathtaking wonder. Only hardship and erosion, or the sculptor's chisel, can release it.

Foundations | 3

GLOBAL POLITICS CAN SOMETIMES HAVE unexpected, and very local, side effects. I guess it's a bit like the proverbial butterfly flapping its wings over the Indian Ocean and causing a tornado in Kentucky. Events that seem remote and impersonal can cause tidal waves in the lives of very small people.

Take the case of Josef, for example, who lived in Berlin during and after the time of the Communist regime in the former East Germany. He was just a humble citizen who, like many of his generation, became disenchanted with the way things were going in his home country. Along with many thousands of others, he decided to make a break for the West. He packed his bags and made his escape, leaving behind just a small, well-tended garden in the heart of the city, where he grew his vegetables and dreamed his dreams.

After Josef's departure, those few square yards of earth sparkled not just with the abundant harvest of beans and cauliflower and cucumbers, but also with the promise of seriously profitable real estate. In short order the state authorities seized the opportunity, appropriated the little garden, and erected no less an edifice upon it than the East German television tower. Authorities were adamant about the specifications: the tower was to be higher than the Eiffel Tower in Paris but suitably lower than the Moscow television tower!

And that might have been the end of the matter, had the regime not collapsed a quarter of a century later, at which point the humble gardener returned to take possession of his vegetable plot once more, only to find it occupied by the huge bulk of the national television tower. The ensuing clash of wills has been keeping the legal profession gainfully employed ever since.

This incident gives me pause. The television tower was built on stolen ground—on a dishonest foundation. What about my own life? Have I built my life on values and principles that are not truly my own? Have I spent my life living someone else's dream? Have other people taken over my heart's soil and used it for their own ends? Have I done this to anyone else?

Is our Western world as a whole built on stolen ground, like that television tower? Have we taken what we desired at the cost of generations still unborn—a profligate present stolen from our children's future? Has the pursuit of our dream of extravagant wealth been the cause of nightmarish poverty elsewhere in the world? Have we constructed our affluent lifestyle on the vegetable plot of our Third-World brothers and sisters, and robbed them of their rightful space in which to grow and flourish?

In the heart of a city under occupation lies a tiny garden, where a man grows his food. In the heart of each of us is a garden where all that is true and genuine within us and among us is seeded and nurtured by God. Let it not be usurped or compromised. It is our Eden.

4 | Shifting Sands

THE SCENE IS THE FORMER YUGOSLAVIA. WE ARE camping beside a river. One of my companions is wading barefoot in the shallow waters, hopping from rock to rock. The rocks are easy to identify, their smooth gray bulk rising above the water's surface. But one of them isn't what it seems. There is a well-camouflaged reptile lying across it. My friend is about to jump onto it when it swims away, expressing its displeasure as it goes!

I make many such leaps of faith as I go through life, trusting that the rock I am trying to land on is solid ground. I have sometimes trusted the rocks of health and wealth, of status and power, of the undisturbed continuance of familiar relationships, career and established "securities," only to find that these footholds have crumbled beneath me. To my detriment, I have learned that such stepping stones are not as reliable as they seem.

Imagine now an innocent-looking sandy beach. The tide is going out, and the sand lies uniformly firm and smooth. But suddenly I find myself up to the ankles in shifting sand. It's a scary moment, and what shocks me most is that there is no way, by merely looking at the sand, to tell where it is truly firm and where it is quicksand. The surface gives no clue as to the possible hazards concealed below.

Our walkways through time are no less deceiving. Sometimes my journey will be safe and sure, and other times it will have the potential to suck me into destructive places and situations. Rarely will I see in advance which paths are which. It calls for constant attentive awareness to notice the destructive suction and step back from it promptly. And this in turn is possible only if I am not obsessed with a blind desire to walk precisely *there,* perhaps because "there" holds some promise of short-term gain or pleasure for me.

How trustworthy are my own foundations? Am I attentive to any signs that the basis of my life may not be as sure as it looks? Am I taking risks and shortcuts that may lead into quicksand?

These are questions for all of us, the whole human family. Urgent questions.

5 | Moments of Truth

I STILL REMEMBER THE DAY, BACK IN 1953, WHEN Mt. Everest was "conquered." At the time there was great rejoicing, as Edmund Hillary and Sherpa Tenzing Norgay set the first human footsteps upon the virgin snows of the mountain's peak. Many years later I heard the story of how differently the two climbers reacted to their achievement: Hillary planted the flag of conquest at the summit, and Tenzing knelt in the snow to beg the mountain's forgiveness for disturbing her peace.

I also remember the day of the first moon landing—a memory indelibly imprinted on the psyche of all who were alive to witness that "small step for man, one giant leap for mankind." Then, too, a flag was placed as a statement of conquest, and great rejoicing broke out, at least in the Western world and especially in the United States. But then too, a new mood was awakened, not of conquest, but of awe and wonder. Later, astronaut Edgar Mitchell would call us all to a deeper level of reflective awareness and collective responsibility as he described his emotions on seeing the earth for the first time from outer space:

" . . . gazing through 240,000 miles of space toward the stars and the planet from which I had come, I suddenly experienced the universe as intelligent, loving, harmonious. . . . My view of our planet was a glimpse of divinity."

These are moments out of time, moments when humankind glimpsed divinity. And when we glimpse divinity, however momentarily, we are forever changed by the encounter. Nothing can ever be the same again.

6 | Grounded

I GIVE THE CAR A TREAT TODAY. IT HASN'T BEEN washed in ages, so I drive it to the local car wash and sit quietly inside it as the machine covers it with suds. Suddenly my familiar world is blotted out. This is not a disagreeable feeling at all. In fact, I luxuriate in my briefly silent, curtained universe. It is like a personal whiteout, and it takes me back to magical childhood days when we used to have proper winters and I would awaken to frosted windows and a crisp and snowbound world.

Whiteouts like this bring a blanket of peace. All sounds are muffled, and every breath seems like a prayer. I am grounded, and when a few minutes have passed I may begin to resent this helplessness. But right now I am so happy to be taken back to a long-buried sense of wonder, stillness, and reverence.

Heaven doesn't last for long—soon I am off and away in my clean car. But those few moments of silent enclosure fuel my whole day.

Grandchild 7

MY GRANDCHILD IS SIX MILLIMETERS LONG TODAY! I gaze at the copy of the first ultrasound image my daughter has given me, the picture in which she and the technicians could see the miniscule heart beating.

Six millimeters of humanity. Just a little cluster of cells throbbing with the overwhelming impulse for life, and packed with unimaginable potential.

I never guessed how much you could love a little cluster of cells.

I never knew how such a tiny being could get inside your deepest dreams, and change things.

8 | Awakening

THE MOMENT IS TIMELESS: STANDING AT MATHER Point on the South Rim of the Grand Canyon, watching the sun rise.

Ever so gently the light spills down the canyon sides, illuminating each hidden crack and crevice with the gold of dawn.

Sometimes our inner awakenings are like that, very gentle, almost imperceptible, so that we hardly realize we are waking up to ourselves. And sometimes they are sudden, like the startled awakening after oversleeping, to discover that we're lying in the full light of a day we never expected.

We don't have to respond, of course. We can choose to turn over and ignore the beckoning light. There are parts of the Grand Canyon that will *never* see the light of day.

Rock Talk | 9

Do rocks have feelings? Is that a silly question? In one sense how could they *not* have feelings?

If they could look up to the stars, they would be gazing at their grandmothers, the source of their being.

If they could look at the myriad life forms teeming around them and upon them they would be gazing at their grandchildren, the countless life forms that have evolved from their primeval solidity.

But rocks cannot gaze as we do. They lack reflective awareness, which is God's gift to *Homo sapiens*. Yet surely that gift, and we ourselves, were bound up inside those rocks, those stars, from the beginning of space-time, until we were released by the midwife of evolution.

Truly we are part of one another—the stars, the rocks, you and I. Yet we alone, upon this planet, are gifted with eyes, hearts, and minds to see the miracle, and to respond.

10 | Sauntering

THE WORD *SAUNTER* EVOKES FOR ME THE SENSE of holy ground, where a pilgrim might linger and reflect on the wonder of life.

I needed a small child to teach me how to saunter. The day had passed by without my realizing it. Soon it would be dinnertime, and the shops would be closing. Hastily I dressed my little girl in her outdoor clothes and rushed off with her to buy some food for a meal.

Rushed? Well no, my child had other ideas. All at once I felt a tug on my hand. Her silent request for a pause in the onward rush was insistent. The journey was well and truly stalled, as she guided me with implacable determination to the edge of the sidewalk, to gaze in rapture as a beetle crossed the road. She was watching this wonder for the first time in her life. She was teaching me to do the same.

I needed a little child to read the map of this world's holy ground and to make me take off my shoes as I tread its sacred pathways through the ordinariness of every day.

All ground reveals its holiness, if I walk upon it with gentleness and mindfulness. God is in every particle.

11 | The Anthill

THE MIGHTY MONOLITH OF ULURU (OFTEN CALLED Ayers Rock) in Central Australia is spirituality in solid form. Every crack and crevice has been sanctified by countless sacred ceremonies carried out there by the local Anangu people. Every fissure and formation tells a story, and every story conveys a meaning, an inspiration, a law, an example, a piece of history.

Uluru didn't rise up from the earth in a dramatic volcanic eruption, nor was it forced skyward by shifting tectonic plates. Rather, the surrounding land sank, or eroded, and exposed the bedrock. It strikes me as nature's parable of our own egos. The true self, the bedrock of our being, emerges through time and experience as the illusory world of the ego gradually erodes away. And the more the true self of each of us emerges, the more we will discover that at the core of our being we are united in the heart of the mystery of God.

Today, Western tourists still insist on clambering over this mighty rock, deaf to the pleas of the Aboriginal people to respect its holiness and walk around the base instead. The local people look on from their tribal lands as, daily, the miniscule figures climb onward and upward. "Look at the ant people," they say. But they speak in sorrow, not in anger. Their chief concern is not so much for the sacrilege being committed on their holy ground as for the risk of injury and death to the climbers. "When someone dies on the rock," they tell us, "we grieve for them. We feel responsible for them."

And we, the ant people, although we might desist from climbing a sacred mountain, still spend most of our waking moments tending our ego-worlds. Do we understand that there is an Uluru in each of us—a bed-rock place where we stand face-to-face with our true self and with the author of our being? Why else do we flock to such liminal places and gaze in silent wonder as the sun rises and sets on a rock in the desert, casting its ever-changing light and shadow over everything we are?

12 | Starlight Dreaming

HERE IS A STAR-FILLED NIGHT IN THE MIDDLE OF the desert. I wake briefly and gaze up through the tent roof at the Milky Way, which spans the heavens immediately overhead. The stars are like sparks from a celestial campfire, and yet here we stand, the children of just one such spark. Even more amazing, we have the ability to reflect on these immense mysteries so much greater than ourselves.

Every possibility and potentiality of God's Great Dream was present in the first sparks of the flaring forth of our universe. The supernova deaths of their ancestors, the first generation stars, ten billion years ago, flung forth all the elements that now form the bedrock of our planet and the bodies of all the creatures on this earth. The rocks surrounding this little camping ground are the grandchildren of the stars and our own grandparents. In a very real way, every living thing was locked up in the Dreamtime of these rocks.

Will the story continue to unfold? If so, what unguessed-at manifestations of that Dream are still locked up inside ourselves? And how will they come to birth?

Will they lead to transcendence, or will they be stillborn? Can we become more than we dare to dream, more fully human, more close to God and to each other, or does the future spell only extinction? Perhaps the choice is ours.

13 | Same River, Fresh Water

I HAVE JUST SPENT A WEEKEND WITH A FRIEND WHO used to be a classmate of mine. We first met before we were five years old, nearly sixty years ago.

Since then, every cell in our bodies has changed, many times over. Not a particle of us remains the same. There's not a thought in our minds that is not in constant flux within a fluid universe.

And yet, when we met last weekend, we still recognized each other as if we had never been apart. In a deep way we were still the same people who first linked hands in the schoolyard all those years ago.

It is said that you can keep going back to the same river but you will never see the same water twice. The converse is also true. The water may change moment by moment, but the river is constant.

If I know my friend, however much she changes, and she knows me, how much more shall we be known, through all our flux, by the author of our being?

My African Great-Grandmother

14

THE ASSISTANT AT THE HUMAN GENOME PROJECT AT the University of Witwatersrand in Johannesburg takes a sample of my DNA and shows me what a cell looks like—just a black pinprick suspended in the test tube. Just a pinprick, yet it contains all the coded information about who I, uniquely, am. I gaze at it in silent amazement. Six weeks later, that cell will have revealed the original source of my mitochondrial DNA—the part of our DNA that passes, unchanged (except for occasional mutations) down the maternal line, from generation to generation.

Like all of us, I am descended from one of the seven lines of our original humanity in East Africa. I am the distant great-grandchild of one of these "seven daughters of Eve." In his book, *The Seven Daughters of Eve*, Brian Sykes, of Oxford University, has assigned names to these seven lines of descent. My own great-grandmother is Helena, and I share her with about forty-seven percent of native

Europeans. Her name means "light." I am deeply moved by that fact and sense the stirring of a desire to live true to her name.

The seed of who I am lay there in East Africa when *Homo sapiens* were just beginning the great adventure of becoming fully human.

Each of these seven lines has meandered through the world, leaving its genetic trail in living evidence of an ancient story. The story has one beginning. In the mystery of our beginnings, we are one.

NORTHEAST

Finding God in All Things

In a story by Anthony de Mello, a fish is searching for the ocean. Everyone he asks has heard of this thing called "ocean," but no one has any idea of what it looks like, or where it might be found. Maybe it is just a figment of fish imagination. Maybe it is just wishful thinking. Or maybe it is the ultimate reality in which every fish lives and moves and has its being. Maybe it is the mystery that nourishes every fish and sea creature and keeps them alive and growing. Maybe it is the place in which every little stirring of the water, every hidden current guides the course of every fish, from the smallest plankton to the mighty whale. Maybe it is the one true home.

If you too are searching for this elusive ocean in which you live and move and have your being, then look no further than what is all around you. God is closer to us than we are to ourselves, so close that we can't see the ocean for the water, the forest for the trees. God is closer to us than our own breathing, closer than our eyes can focus, less than a heartbeat away.

Where will we find this mysterious presence that is so close yet seems so far away? As we head northeast, we discover that God is, quite simply, everywhere, in all that happens and in every particle of all that is.

Enjoy your exploration every day. Read the sermons in the stones along your path. Listen to the song that daily life is singing in your heart. Find God around the next turn in the road, just waiting to surprise you.

Jam Tomorrow | 15

IT HAS BEEN A LONG WEEK. I AM FEELING QUITE TIRED as I climb into the taxi that will take me on the first stage of my journey home from the retreat house where I have been working. I am also anxiously thinking back over all that has transpired, wondering whether I "got it right," whether the retreatants were satisfied with their experience and how it has left them feeling.

I say my good-byes to the people there who welcomed me so warmly and supported me so generously. Such good-byes are a regular feature of my life these days, and they are double-edged. On the one hand I know that for the people who give me hospitality I am just a temporary guest; there is no real permanence and the journey moves on. On the other hand I know that those whose lives connect, however briefly, remain in some deep sense connected forever. If a place has been my home for a week, then at some level it will always be my home.

We approach the town and round a bend to head up to the station. There on the corner stands a pub that catches my eye—not because it is especially scenic, but on account of the notice painted boldly above the door: "Free beer tomorrow—for anyone who missed it yesterday."

It makes me smile. Of course, you would wait forever for your free beer! Actually, that little sign is more than a reason to chuckle. It shakes me from my wondering over past events and places and reminds me that the here-and-now is the only reality. It reminds me that in fact I spend most of my time and energy anticipating the free beer (or, more often, the problems) that might come tomorrow, or fretting about the opportunities I missed yesterday.

Live in the *now,* that silly pub sign says to me. Drink deeply of today.

Accidental Epiphanies | 16

THE TRAIN TRUNDLES ITS LEISURELY WAY THROUGH the English Midlands. I have a good book, and, for once, time to read it. I immerse myself and give little thought to the passing landscape until, a couple of hours into the journey, for no apparent reason I suddenly feel the urge to put the book down and look at the world outside. A huge white horse, carved out of the chalky soil and offset by the lush green grass of the surrounding hillside, greets my astonished gaze. I know that these artifacts exist in various parts of the British Isles. But I certainly didn't expect to see one right here in the middle of nowhere, easily visible from the train.

I stare at the equine work of art, and in just a few seconds it disappears from view behind a range of hills; I expect never to see it again. I realize that I have had my unscheduled glimpse of it in just the few moments it was visible from the train, and I feel unaccountably grateful, both to the people who carved it and to the God who has prompted me into awareness at precisely the right moment. A good spirit whispers in my ear, "Discover the wonder of the moment, and know that unguessed-at beauty lies just below the surface of everything and everyone you meet."

At the next stop, a well-dressed young man boards the train and settles in across the aisle, and almost before we leave the station, he is fast asleep. At first I take no notice, but after we have passed a few stations, I begin to wonder whether he might sleep through his stop. At Birmingham he suddenly wakes up, asks me where we are, seems satisfied with the answer, and goes back to sleep again. I marvel at his ability to relax and let himself be carried. But I also notice that the ticket he has left lying at his side is issued to Crewe. I make a mental note to wake him when we reach Crewe, but again, I needn't have worried. He wakes spontaneously and alights without a care in the world. And again the good spirit smiles and asks me, "Can *you* risk being so childlike in your trust? Can *you* fall asleep in God's arms and entrust yourself to God's guiding of the journey?"

I'm discovering that every journey has little epiphanies to reveal. The real miracle, however, isn't that there are epiphanies along the way, but that the way itself is a continuous epiphany. God is waiting to reveal love and wisdom in every step. I need only eyes to see the moments of wonder and ears to register the whispers of wisdom.

17 | The Restaurant Bird

ON A TINY CORAL ISLAND ON THE GREAT BARRIER Reef, about seventy miles off the coast of Eastern Australia, there lives a little bird. I don't even know his name. I met him during a stay on that island a few years ago. More precisely, I was introduced to him by a local guide, who called him simply "the restaurant bird." These sturdy little birds have lived on that island for as long as anyone can remember. They feed on whatever they can scavenge from the restaurant. In fact, they enjoy the good life out there, and, as everyone on the island well knows, they are completely flightless! Well, who would fly anywhere, when there is a gourmet meal three times a day at the restaurant?

But one day someone had the bright idea of colonizing another reef island with these complacent and easy-going birds. A consignment of them was packed in crates and taken by boat to a neighboring uninhabited island, some forty miles away, where they were duly deposited in their new home. The next morning these "flightless" birds were all back outside the restaurant on their native soil, waiting for breakfast.

When God offers us life in all its fullness, will we rise above our limitations as eagerly as an exiled restaurant bird? Or will we stay locked in our conviction that we are utterly incapable of flight, or as we might express it, trapped in our learned dependency? Desires are powerful. They are stronger than all the things we think we can't do!

18 | Nothing but the Truth

In Poland, storks are a common sight, and local people believe that they bring good luck. In their enthusiasm for these birds, people sometimes decorate their chimneys with plastic stork replicas. But what catches my eye today is a particular, very real stork sitting astride the ridge of a rooftop, pecking angrily at a plastic replica of himself and furiously throwing down pieces of the impostor to the street below.

What a discerning creature. And what a lesson he is teaching me. He will not tolerate the inauthentic. He insists on the real thing, and nothing less!

What about me, I wonder?

When I glimpse the image of my less-than-authentic self, reflected in the baubles of a consumer culture or in my own superficial wants and wishes, how will my true and deepest self react? What will I do with all that's within me that is not real? Am I ready to shed those layers of my life that are concerned with acquisition, achievement, security, popularity, and so many other desires that have no real weight? Am I ready to let these things be stripped away, and to trust that what is left will be the real me, my true self?

Will my heart know the difference between God's Dream and the world's many plastic replicas?

19 | A Child's First Snowflake

THE DOUBLE-DECKER BUS LURCHES TO A HALT AT the bus stop. On the top deck a little boy begs to be allowed to descend the stairs on his own. Father refuses and picks up the toddler. And all hell breaks loose. The other passengers sigh with relief as the man carries the screaming child off the bus.

Then, just as father and son step onto the sidewalk, it begins to snow. The frustrated child looks up and sees the first snowflakes drifting down, and, mouth still wide open and ready to emit the next wail, he falls silent and gazes in pure joy at the falling snow.

The sheer wonder at the loveliness of the world far outweighs my minor frustrations. May I have the grace to know it, and to respond as that child did.

Stories in Stones | 20

I have a little bag of pebbles. They're so attractive that I use them as visual aids for retreats and workshops.

One day during a retreat in Ireland, I spread out the stones on a table. To my delight, one morning I find two of the participants poring over them, handling them as if they were diamonds, and marveling to one another.

When I express my surprise, they explain that they have been missionaries in Zimbabwe, and that many of these pebbles come from that part of the world. They tell me how they used to collect them from ancient riverbeds. They know every one of them by name and can tell me all about it.

Just a bag of pebbles to me. But to them, each one has a name and a story.

Just like people. We see the anonymous crowds, but they are made up of unique individuals, beloved and beautiful, each carrying a sacred story.

21 | Hadeda

There is a raucous South African bird called the hadeda. You can hear hadedas a mile away. They screech at dawn and shatter your slumbers. You imagine that they must be voracious, aggressive creatures.

At least that's what I thought—until one afternoon when I'm having tea with a friend in Johannesburg. He points to a bird walking peacefully across his lawn—a hadeda. "Look at its eyes," he urges me.

I look, and what I see are the gentlest of eyes gazing back at me—perhaps a little apprehensive of this stranger—but calm. And, ultimately, so gentle.

Perhaps we see the gentle heart of another person only when we risk going beyond the raucous exterior and getting close enough to look into his eyes.

Local Connections | 22

I ALWAYS GET A TREMOR OF EXCITEMENT WHEN THE single-car, country train comes trundling into the local station. Sometimes it hardly looks as though it will make it to the platform, let alone to the nearby city to which it will carry us.

But it does! The journey takes only ten minutes, but without that shaky little train I would never reach the hub of rail connections that will carry me anywhere in the country, and to the airports from which I can fly all over the world.

My prayer is like that: shaky, slow, seemingly unreliable, and going nowhere fast. But if I can just entrust myself to it, it will take me way beyond my own thoughts and powers.

The smallest, most tenuous of connections links us to the depth of the Mystery. When I pray, I step on board that little country train, and there are no limits to where it may lead.

23 | Eucharist

The Spirit blows where she will, especially it seems through the lives of many people who would say they are not religious, yet who are doing the very things that Jesus did. They are leaving behind a comfortable lifestyle and going out to the poorest people in the world to help them grow food and build schools. They are campaigning for justice in an unjust world. They are tending sick or elderly neighbors or teaching disadvantaged children.

They are giving their lives in the care of others, pouring out their energy for the sake of peace and justice, yet they would never guess that they are being blessed and broken, and given for the world.

They would never guess that they are Eucharist. They are the living presence in the world of the communion bread and wine upon the altar.

Eucharist, perhaps, is not something to be reserved in a holy place, but *spent,* not something we are asked to worship, but something we are invited to *become.* And just as in Jesus' day, sometimes we see this in action where we absolutely don't expect it, and we find it lacking in some of the places where it is supposed to be permanently resident.

24 | Evening Primrose

THE EVENING PRIMROSE NEVER FAILS TO AMAZE me. IN their season, the flowers open up about half an hour before sunset, and when they do it's like watching time-lapse photography, a nature documentary on fast-forward. The bud suddenly splits open and the petals unfurl in minutes, before your eyes.

But this flower has a short life. Twenty-four hours later it will be withering and dying. Just one day of life—one day that may be lived in glorious sunshine or in fog, rain, wind, or storm. Just one day, to give delight and to release its seed upon the earth.

It gives me courage to live my rather longer human life with that kind of trustful surrender. Some of us get a life in the sunshine of love, security, happiness, health, and success. Others struggle with sickness, poverty, failure, and disappointment and never get a glimpse of happiness. Yet every life matters and leaves a little seed.

We can't change the weather of our circumstances. We can only shape the seed that our lives pass on to those who come after us.

Knowing, Understanding, Forgiving

25

THE LAME MAN STANDS ON THE OUTSIDE OF THE revolving door, gathering up his small store of energy to tackle the challenge of getting into the building. As he is just about ready to do so, another man approaches the revolving door from the inside, swings himself through it, and brushes past the lame man waiting unsteadily outside.

Their shoulders touch, and the slight pressure causes the lame man to lose his balance and stumble, losing his hard-won position. He will have to begin the task all over again.

The other man seems not to notice the magnitude of what has just happened but walks on with just a murmured, "Sorry."

The lame man follows the other's departing tracks with a hurt and angry gaze, before beginning to gather himself again. Suppressed rage and frustration show clearly on his face.

He does not realize that the man who has brushed past him so carelessly is blind.

To know all is to understand all: to understand all is to forgive all.

I begin to see why Jesus warns us not to judge.

Teen Static | 26

I LISTEN WITH MOUNTING FRUSTRATION TO THE CAR radio AS it tries to find a transmitter. All I hear are static and interference, as it surfs the dial in search of a signal.

I have the same feeling of dissonance at the beginning of a concert when the orchestra is tuning up.

Both remind me of the challenge of living with teenagers, who seem to do nothing but fizzle and crackle and emit discordant noises.

And I begin to realize that this is inevitable during those years when they are seeking out their natural frequency. I know, too, that the one who seeks her true frequency, whatever the resulting noise and discord may be, is dearer to me by far than the one who settles for whatever station happens to be on and never tests the possibilities.

I hope that I will have the patience to let the young people around me find their own way in life, their own destiny, even if they make a lot of noise about it. Better by far to become who they truly are, however stormy that process may be, than to settle for becoming only the person other people think they ought to be.

The Love of a Child | 27

The main street through the little market town is surprisingly empty. On Wednesdays, stores close at noon. But the fleeting sense of restfulness is shattered by a strident adult voice and the undercurrent of a child's whimpering.

The little family scurries along the street. The mother is beside herself with rage. Three small children run alongside her and behind her, trying to keep up with her angry strides. One, a small boy of six or seven, is the object of her wrath. His face streams with tears and his eyes are desperate with bewilderment and fear. His mother's words freeze on the air: "Just go! Get away from me! I don't care where you go. Just go!"

I know the force of fury that a recalcitrant child can provoke. Yet this mother's damning rejection causes my heart to shrivel up in solidarity with her little son's impotent misery. I feel as if I have witnessed a scene out of hell.

I walk on for awhile, shocked by the blast of negative energy that has just passed by. Then a flashback takes me by surprise—it's a scene from years ago when my daughter was about the age of that little boy. I can see the gray surface of the school playground with its hopscotch squares. I can see the high windows in the Victorian school building and the door opening to let out the class of seven-year-olds at half past three.

This remembered scene reminds me all too painfully of the many times I lost my own patience as a parent, and—amazingly—of how often my daughter nevertheless came hurtling across the schoolyard, hair flying and satchel trailing in the dust, throwing herself at me and burying me in the torrent of her day's news.

Can it be that a child's forgiveness can be even stronger than a parent's wrath? Can it be that the God, who holds both parental fury and child-like love in an ultimately healing embrace, is bigger than all of it.

Bricks and Bubbles | 28

It's a sunny summer morning in Loyola, Spain, birthplace of Ignatius Loyola. I stroll through the little park in front of the imposing basilica and sit on a bench to enjoy the warmth. Behind me rises the imposing basilica, swathed in scaffolding while extensive repairs are being carried out. In front of me is a little kiosk selling newspapers, cigarettes, and other sundries.

A man appears with his little daughter and their dog. He buys a newspaper for himself and a bottle of soap bubbles for the little girl. He sits down to read while she plays happily, blowing her bubbles into the bright blue sky. She rejoices visibly over each new globe with its vibrant colors, and its secret dream world. To her, each bubble is a universe. Wonder is written all over her face. For the dog, the bubbles are toys to be caught between his teeth. He jumps after them and occasionally manages to catch one. But as soon as he does, it dissolves into the air.

I learn more in ten minutes from this scene than from hours on my knees in the basilica. I learn something important about the wonder of our being, about its extreme fragility, and about how as soon as we try to contain and control it, we lose it.

Stripes | 29

WHEN A ZEBRA FOAL IS BORN, SO THE RANGER informs me, it first staggers to its feet and runs in circles round its mother's legs. Nature's way, no doubt, of getting those spindly newborn limbs strong enough, quickly enough, to flee from predators.

But then, exhausted, the newborn foal collapses in a weary heap and lies back, simply gazing, for hours it seems, at its mother. *How very cute,* I think. But this isn't cuteness; it's something else altogether. This is the foal memorizing its mother's stripe pattern.

Imagine! Every single zebra on this planet has a unique stripe pattern. Memorizing its mother's pattern is the foal's first act of bonding, its first defense against getting lost in the herd.

I believe that God paints a unique pattern of presence in each human life. We discover this pattern as we reflect on what is actually happening in our everyday experience. It is there we will notice God's personal relationship with us, unfolding minute by minute.

This reflection becomes an attitude of mindfulness, an ongoing act of bonding, and it holds us in an unbreakable connection with the source of our being through every moment of our living.

EAST

Probing the Darkness

DARKNESS. IS IT JUST THE EMPTY, FRUITLESS TIME between dusk and dawn? The place of ignorance where we have no signs by which to steer our course? The measure of our own lack of enlightenment, our profound need of God?

Do we see it more readily in others than in ourselves? Can we believe that God is also in the darkness with us, alongside us, perhaps especially in the times when we cannot see our own hand in front of our eyes? Can we recognize God as that unfailing presence that, usually, we can see only with the gift of hindsight?

But things grow in the darkness: seeds, bulbs, dreams, babies. Can we trust that if we dare to probe the darkness we may discover things about ourselves that we might prefer not to know, but need to learn? Can we believe that the seeds of all we can become are already gestating in the darkness we would gladly deny?

In the East, a new dawn waits just below the horizon.

Prayer Planting | 30

THE ARRIVAL OF AUTUMN AWAKENS MY URGE TO plant bulbs in my tiny backyard, which is bravely trying to exist on a layer of builders' rubble. I wonder if a few daffodil bulbs will survive in such hostile terrain. For a while, that is as far as my good intentions go. The bulbs sit in their bags, while I engage with the world in a variety of other ways. This is a bit like prayer can be, really. The good intentions are there, and even some degree of preparation. But when push comes to shove, almost anything, however trivial, can intervene and claim a higher place on my list of priorities.

Then, one morning, I am reading Anne Lamott's *Plan B* and come upon her comment that bulbs are prayer too. Bulbs! She must have been reading my mind. Maybe my bulbs, still hanging there in the bag, will open that creaky gate to prayer. With renewed enthusiasm I get out the trowel and the fork and get started on my unpromising backyard.

My first discovery, when I finally spread the bulbs out on the grass in preparation for burial, is that a few of them have started to go moldy. These, especially, remind me of issues in my life that I seem incapable of either dealing with appropriately myself, or, more sensibly, surrendering into God's hands. Instead, they just hang around, like a bad smell, becoming more putrid with each passing day. I pick up the offending bulbs, wipe the green sheen from their outer skins, and lay them with as much gentleness as I can into the hole I've dug for them. In my heart I try to lay to rest some of the life issues as well, trying to convince myself that I really do believe in resurrection and transformation.

The remaining bulbs follow. Down into the darkness. Will there be a resurrection? Will these little specks of incipient life actually blossom out of this unlikely soil? With every bulb, a little dream, a little hope is buried too. With a little anxiety. I cover them all with a layer of the compost of trust, and there they lie in God's hands. For now, there's nothing more I can do.

Broken Shell | 31

WE ARE IN A HALF-FORGOTTEN WAR CEMETERY deep IN central Germany, searching for the grave of a young boy who died in one of the last battles around Berlin at the end of the Second World War. He was fifteen when he was killed by a Soviet tank. He was trying to defend his homeland with a stick.

We find his grave, stark and silent among many thousands more—and bare, except for one small detail. A tiny, sky-blue egg has fallen from a bird's nest in an overhanging branch. The shell lies there, still unbroken, perfect, yet robbed of its chance of life, on the grave—the shell of a bird that will never sing, never fly, never become what God has dreamed it might be. And I weep for the boy who will never grow up. A unique and indispensable part of God's Dream lies in the earth, beneath that broken shell. And our inhumanity has callously dispensed with it.

I think of the millions who now lie in cold graves throughout the world because they were dispatched to the killing fields. Every one of them has a story. Every one of them is priceless in God's eyes. We remember them each autumn, in sorrow and in shame as well as with the pride and reverence they deserve. And we remember not only those who died, but those who must continue living, carrying the trauma of war and violence in their bodies, minds, and souls. Their stories have been disfigured brutally by the kind of experience no human should ever know.

When we align ourselves with with violence, we rob life of its potential to come to birth. We abort a part of God's Dream.

Yet God's Dream is greater than anything we can do in opposition to it. God's light has pierced the darkness, and the darkness has *not* extinguished it. How does this make any sense under the shadow of all our warmongering, and under the cloud of all our loss and grieving? What hope might there be for *kindling* light, rather than extinguishing it?

Empire State | 32

CAN ONE LITTLE LIGHT MAKE ANY DIFFERENCE IN the darkness?

On my first visit to New York City, I go to the top of the Empire State building late one night. When the elevator reaches the topmost viewing platform, I step out and gaze down on a breathtakingly beautiful view. I'm not the only one to be awed by the sight. A group of youngsters who have chattered all the way up immediately fall into a wide-eyed silence as they step onto the platform. Everyone is blown away by the sea of beauty sparkling at our feet. The city is alive with light.

But exactly how has this spectacle come about? It isn't some lavish Hollywood show, put on to draw the crowds. It is simply the result of millions of ordinary people switching on the lights in their own apartments. None of them will have thought for a moment that they are contributing to a vision that can take your breath away.

One small light can kindle a fire that changes the world.

God's vast visions always begin with the little ones, as the gospel keeps reminding us. *We* are the little people. The light of life is given to *us*. When we light a candle, we say to the darkness, "I beg to differ."

The Cost of Unhealthy Dependence | 33

IN THE WOODS, I STOP BESIDE AN ANCIENT OAK TREE. I can hardly see its bark, it's so completely swathed in clinging ivy, from its roots to its crown. I wonder how the tree feels! Maybe the ivy feels like a cozy comforter, shielding the tree from the winter weather. Does the oak ever guess that what seems to be wrapping it in comfort is in fact slowly, relentlessly, suffocating it?

I walk on, uncomfortably, remembering some of my own blankets, my own unhealthy dependencies, and remember a story.

There once was a little bird with pretty feathers. And there was a wily fox. Every day the bird dug for a worm to eat. Eventually the fox made her an offer she couldn't refuse. "I can get you a worm every day, and you wouldn't have to do all this digging," he suggested.

"All I ask in return is that you give me just one of your beautiful feathers each day. A worm for a feather. Do we have a deal?"

This very neat arrangement went on happily for a long time. The bird had a perfect meal ticket. And the fox?

One day the bird had no more feathers left to give, nor any to fly away with. And the fox enjoyed a special meal that day.

Candles of Mass Destruction

34

THE X-RAY MACHINE AT THE AIRPORT REVEALS AN unexplained object in my carry-on baggage. We go through the usual routine. Is this my bag? Yes! Did I pack it myself? Yes! The security official conscientiously unpacks every item, one by one.

The culprit is a little candle holder—a gift for a friend. There's no problem with the ceramic holder, but a tiny tea light offends and is confiscated. The official explains that explosives could have been mixed into the wax. We look at each other in mutual disbelief at the absurdity of it all, but he has his orders.

I proceed to the boarding gate, wondering what is happening to a world that feels threatened by a little Christmas candle.

The light shines in the darkness. Let not our irrational fears become the darkness that extinguishes it.

35 | A Thin, Thin Line

A FLASH OF ANGER CAN BE THE HEALING SPARK that releases suppressed tensions, or it can be the first step that unleashes a terrible argument.

A blind eye and a deaf ear can be a mark of tolerance and understanding, or the sign of a cowardly refusal to speak out in the face of injustice.

A well-meaning friend can smother others with his efforts at helpfulness, and actually rob them of their freedom to choose their own course and make their own mistakes.

Such a thin line divides healing from harm, the creative from the destructive spirit within us.

Privacy and secrecy are close neighbors. Loving support walks almost hand-in-hand with domination. Tolerance rubs shoulders with apathy.

There are no maps.

Just the quiet of a peaceful heart, where, maybe, a little light might glow to show the way.

Adapted to Crookedness? | 36

MY FRIEND HAS SUFFERED ALL HER LIFE FROM the effects of a crooked spine, often carrying a bed with her to lie on when sitting became too painful.

Only now, in later life, is she learning that her pain comes not from her spine, but from all the muscles that have adapted themselves to its crookedness and thus become strained and distorted.

The power of this parable isn't lost on her, or on me. How much of our pain—in society, in the church, or in the family—comes from our attempts to fit in with what is in fact distorted in itself? How much anguish comes from our collusions with falsehood?

Re-educating the muscles is also a painful process, but in the end it will be the only true choice.

37 | Rules

IT HAS BEEN SAID THAT RULES ARE NEEDED BY THOSE who have lost their inner balance, and also by those who have not yet discovered it.

I wonder where we as the human race lie along this spectrum. Have we lost a wisdom we once possessed? Or have we not yet discovered it?

Does Jesus save us from the follies of the past, or does he lead and guide us toward a fullness of wisdom and love that still lies beyond us?

Are we offenders who need correction, or infants who need to be nurtured into maturity?

For Sale: First Place in Line

38

It's a long transit between terminals at Heathrow. In front of me on one of the escalators stands a woman towing her carry-on baggage, to which is attached a label announcing that she is a member of the Priority Club.

This grates on me, maybe simply because I don't have such privilege. But mainly, I think, because of the absurdity of thinking that we should be able to buy priority, purchase advantages over our fellow human beings.

It grates on me because of course it is true. I live in a culture that habitually buys privilege over others—over whole nations and continents of others. The thought disturbs and dislocates my comfortable padding of complacency.

Maybe we don't realize the injustice of a world in which money buys privilege and bestows power—until we come up against those who have purchased an advantage over *us*.

At times such as these, we should listen to that still, small voice that once said, "The first shall be last."

Focusing the Light | 39

Are we really allowing the light of Christ to banish our darkness, or are we using it to target each other more accurately when we aim our sectarian arrows? Do we think we glorify God when we diminish and demonize each other?

When we insist that our own particular way of worship or service is superior to any other are we not eclipsing the light of Christ with our own ego-selves? When we dare to dismiss another spiritual tradition as misguided, or refuse to sit down together with those of other persuasions, are we really serving the gospel in which we say we believe?

May we use the Christ-light to reveal the pain in each other, and not to more accurately inflict it?

40 | The Freedom Cage

A FAMILY IN SOUTH AFRICA HAS A LITTLE HOLIDAY home on the coast, to which they retreat regularly. However, close by are baboons, potentially dangerous creatures, and they are becoming not just a nuisance, but a threat—so much so that the family erects a little cage-like shelter on the beach, where they can sit in the sun, safe from the incursions of the baboons.

The image of this holiday cage raises big questions: about freedom and captivity, about prey and predator, about thinking we own the world and discovering that we don't even own ourselves. About realizing that we survive and thrive only by permission of God, the universe, and one another.

Perhaps this situation is an illustration of the African phrase, *ubuntu*—"I am because you are." No one exists in isolation, but only in a vast network of interrelationship and interdependency.

It's worth remembering, too, that what we think is freedom might actually be a cage.

The New Suit

41

A LITTLE STORY COMES MY WAY, ONE THAT MAKES me think, in quite a powerful way, about how easily we adapt ourselves to other people's values, even when those values are patently false.

An upstanding young man goes to a tailor to have a suit custom made. The tailor, delighted to have a new customer, eagerly takes the young man's measurements and brings out samples of his best cloth from which his client is invited to choose. A material of the most excellent quality is duly selected and the work begins.

Several weeks pass, and the young man is summoned for the first fitting of the new suit. He tries it on and realizes that it seems to be pulling across the shoulders. "No problem," says the tailor. "You just need to bend sideways a bit more." Another week passes, and another fitting. The young man has never actually had a suit custom made before, and he doesn't like to appear too critical, so he hunches himself into the jacket. This time one sleeve is clearly longer than the other. He points this out to the tailor. "No problem," says the tailor. "You only need to hold the shorter sleeve down a bit with your hand, and then they will both look the same length." Again, the young man doesn't like to argue, and so complies with this bizarre suggestion.

Finally come the trousers. Getting into the trousers is such a struggle that the young man can't rightly see how he is ever going to be able to walk in them, but the tailor surveys him admiringly. "My word, sir, but you cut a fine figure in this suit." The client smiles wanly and limps across the room, trying not to look too closely at his reflection in the mirror. With reluctance, and in deep disappointment over the suit project, he pays the bill and hobbles home.

On his way home, people in the street turn to stare at him as he advances like a crab in the lopsided trousers, his shoulders painfully crooked, and holding one sleeve down with his hand. "Poor guy," says one of the bystanders. "What a shame that such a young man should be so deformed. But how lucky he is to have such a skillful tailor!"

Do I have the courage to be myself, and to resist the attempts of other people or institutions to make me adapt to a mold I was never intended to fit? The cost of false adaptation may be crippling.

Progress, Written Backward

42

JOHN CALLS THIS MORNING TO DO SOME REPAIR work in my home. I tell him about my recent travels, and we get to talking about the problems of air travel and airport expansion.

His eyes grow misty as he remembers his childhood in Manchester, close to what has now become a rapidly expanding international airport. He tells me that Mrs. Griffin, who lived nearby, used to take the local children out for long country walks around the fields that have now become runways. How they used to relish these expeditions! The children would gather berries in the fall, and their elderly friend would make jam for everyone.

Now the local children are mainly confined to their homes, as the world is no longer a safe playground. Now, if any berries could still grow, they would be saturated in aviation fuel. Now the airport even charges a fee for children to stand and watch the aircraft starting and landing.

John muses that, in return, we have "progress." Business travelers, who could easily conduct their meetings by conference phone and who don't have to pay their own travel expenses, ply the skies with abandon. Holiday-makers, who have lost their local oases to new building developments, now fly thousands of miles in search of substitutes. Green fields morph into parking lots, and jam is flown in from the other side of the world. Children, whose grandparents roamed the fields and knew every plant and berry growing there, no longer know where berries come from, if not from the supermarket shelves.

And underneath it all we experience, not just a longing for times lost, but also an abiding sorrow for the legacy of which our grandchildren have been robbed.

We can cross the Atlantic in the time it used to take Mrs. Griffin to make her winter jam. But are we richer or poorer for the progress we have made? Is it time to stop, and think?

Solitary Confinement | 43

On a free afternoon in Kingston, Ontario, I take a bus ride to explore the harbor and downtown area. It's a beautiful day, and I relish my hours in the sun, puttering around Kingston's historic past and strolling the Philosopher's Walk, a lakeside pathway designed to be as straight as possible so that wandering students, lost in thought, might safely walk there without falling into Lake Ontario.

The time comes to get the bus back home, and I settle down for the twenty-minute ride. A young couple takes the seat in front of me, their small baby in a carrier snuggled between them. The little one is fast asleep, pacifier in her mouth. I am fascinated, and gaze at her as she sleeps.

Then I notice that the parents—though perfectly good and caring, I'm sure—seem unaware of the miracle that lies between them. Each of them extracts a cell phone and, in his and her own private world, plays a private game on the flickering little screen.

The baby wakes and pushes the pacifier away. Her gaze meets mine. What a moment her parents are missing, as those little blue eyes light up at the wonder of this new experience, this ride in a bus—this moving, challenging, wonderful world.

Strange, how the miracle of the *more* in life can lie unnoticed because it is buried under layers and layers of the *less*. And ironic, that the technology designed to extend our powers of communication can also seduce us into becoming islands of solitary confinement.

SOUTHEAST

Following the Dream

THERE ARE THOSE WHO SAY LIFE IS SIMPLY A VALE OF tears, to be got through with the minimum of pain and effort. There are others who believe in something worth following—something they probably couldn't really define if they are honest. They would say that, because they feel so strongly the impulse to follow this dream, this is a sign in itself that there is indeed a dream to follow. And then again there are others who know that they don't really know, but choose in any case to live their lives as though their lives have meaning. This choice, in itself, actually does give their lives meaning.

The sun has risen in the east. The noon hour is near, but not yet. We turn southeast. Will we see the dream rising with the sun, and if we see it, will we follow into the midday hour?

Only if the Dream walks along with us, before and behind us, to our left and our right, and not if we lock the dream away in a golden box on a high pedestal, marked "Keep out of the reach of children." Maybe children see most clearly the traces of the Dream who is the Way. Maybe that's why Jesus invites us all to become as little children.

Dream Signs | 44

It begins as a normal sort of day, with the routine commute to the office twenty-five miles away. My heart sings just a little, because it's a sunny day, and it's hard to harbor resentment on such a morning, even about having to go to a job every day that never quite touches who I really am or engages who I might become.

The route takes me through spring-arrayed country lanes. I know the way so well I could travel it blind, and maybe mainly I do, but from the corner of my eye a gleam catches my attention, and I slow down. A huge farm horse is grazing at the edge of a field. He lifts his massive head as I approach, and just for a split, shutter-opening second, the sunlight sets his whiskers on fire. Just a silvered bristle, but it strikes into my heart like a shaft of God. It will remain engraved on my soul forever.

On the way home, I negotiate the suburbs of my hometown. The road circles round a grassy bank planted with cherry trees. The May-time blossoms are so thick on them that I can almost taste the cherries. Beneath them a little girl is playing, scooping up the fallen blossoms and throwing them above her head, letting them descend like confetti. Her delight is like the delight of the first morning, when the creating Spirit saw it all and said "This is *good*!" She exults in the blossom with the same joy in which God says Yes! to creation.

Coal into Diamonds | 45

A SPECTACULARLY UNREMARKABLE MAN WALKS haltingly onto the stage DURING a TV talent show. He is visibly apologetic for taking up space on the planet. His head falls slightly to one side as if in a permanent state of deference. His nervous smile reveals a gap created by crooked front teeth, and his arms hang awkwardly at his sides, as though they didn't quite belong to him. His whole appearance exudes a total lack of self-confidence. With eyes shyly reluctant to meet the camera, he hesitantly shares with the nation that he is a cell phone salesman from Cardiff, but his entire demeanor gives off a different message: I'm nobody really, and I don't know what I'm doing here.

A panel of three judges await him. One of them in particular has a reputation for ruthless criticism and is apparently in the mood to live up to it. They roll their eyes in anticipation of what they might be about to sit through—and I too find myself cringing in dread.

Then the man opens his mouth, and the most sublime voice you can imagine pours forth, as though

Pavarotti himself had come back to remind us that nothing ever dies. But this is not Luciano Pavarotti. It is Paul Potts from Cardiff. A stunned silence falls upon the whole scene, broken only by the eruption of tumultuous applause. I feel the hairs rising in the nape of my neck. The cameras zoom in on the judges' faces. One has tears in her eyes. All are spellbound.

Paul sweeps the board and becomes a national hero overnight. A filmed flashback shows him walking along the shore of his native South Wales, revealing that his secret dream has always been to spend his life doing what he feels he was born to do.

The judges also have dreams, it appears. One describes Paul as a little lump of coal who has become a diamond. Another shares the vision they'd all had at the start of the show: that some ordinary, unassuming person, doing a very ordinary job and quite unaware of his extraordinary gifting, might truly discover who he was and become a gift to the world.

Sometimes God's Dream takes aeons of time to emerge out of eternity, and sometimes it happens overnight. It's a Dream about what we are born to do and who we are born to be, an invitation to each of us to become who we are, a unique human fully alive, a shaft of the glory of God.

Paul himself sums it up: "I have always felt insignificant, but now I know I *am* somebody. I am Paul Potts." Who am *I*? Who are *you*? When we can answer that question with both confidence and humility, then we are echoing back something of the very being of God who says, "I am who I am."

46 | Excess Baggage

THE PLANE TOUCHES DOWN IN LAS VEGAS. NEITHER my friend nor I have much of a clue about camping, and so along with the tent, the sleeping bags, and the backpacks, we have packed all kinds of things that "might come in useful," with the result that we can hardly move beyond the carousel.

Along with the mountain of things both needful and needless, however, we carry something both weightless and invisible—an enormous enthusiasm about our upcoming trek into the deserts of Arizona and Utah and also a blessed innocence and ignorance of the possible hazards. We know that this journey is going to be spiritual as well as physical, and we share a hope and a trust that the silence of the desert will speak to our hearts.

We could hardly call ourselves pioneers. We are not the first travelers ever to penetrate the canyon lands. Yet our mountain of baggage is a sharp reminder that the first nonnative pioneers of these lands got here the hard way—in wagon trains, over mountainous obstructions.

They made it only because they learned to travel light and to jettison any excess baggage along the way.

A dream weighs nothing. All it needs is a bit of food and shelter to sustain the human life in which it chooses to be birthed. Already our hearts, if not our bags, are lighter, as we hit the road for canyon country and eat up the miles along Route 66.

47 | GPS Device or Compass?

To hear ourselves talk about God, we might think that God is some kind of satellite navigational aid on life's dashboard. We think that if we listen hard enough we will hear the divine signals coming through: keep right; take the next exit; take a left in half a mile.

But it isn't so easy! We have to make every choice ourselves, but not alone. The wisdom we have is not in some add-on gadget but within us. God's guidance is not a GPS device, but perhaps a compass.

God never promised an easy ride, with all decisions made for us by some divine website in the sky. But God promises to travel with us, every mile of the way, helping us pay attention to the terrain, to notice the signs—to read the compass.

Wandering Roots | 48

Whenever I hear the song from *Evita*, "Another Suitcase in Another Hall," I see myself. My seminomadic life means that I am never really at home anywhere. I am welcomed wherever I go, but that welcome is limited to the few days I will be there. After that, someone else will need my bed, and I must move on.

But being at home nowhere has taught me the amazing truth that actually I can be at home anywhere.

Being a bird of passage, a temporary guest wherever I go, means that I can learn to live much more fully in the present moment, which actually is all there ever is.

It's strange that a sense of wandering homelessness can reveal a deeper rootedness. And being a guest can open up new dimensions of belonging.

49 | The Shot I Never Got

I ENJOY PHOTOGRAPHY. NOT THAT I'M AN EXPERT—far from it. I notice, though, that when I try to capture on film a place, an experience, or a sense of presence that stirs me especially deeply, I always fail spectacularly. The snapshots are invariably very poor reflections of a reality that refuses to be possessed. I have a particularly fine photo of a clump of grass in Scotland from which a magnificent puffin had just flown away, and a whole series of images of South African waters in which (believe me!) the whales were constantly appearing.

If I can't even "capture" a puffin, how would I expect to ever capture a dream?

But, really, I am glad that I fail so consistently, because if I could capture those places or moments, they wouldn't be what they are. Just as, if I could get a handle on "God," God would no longer be mystery, and would no longer be God.

"Lord, I believe. Help my unbelief."

"Lord, I think I know you. Bless my monumental ignorance."

Detours

|50

WHEN THE FREEWAY IS CLOSED, OR SNARLED UP with traffic, I may have to take a detour.

I resent it, and grumble to myself about the waste of time and fuel. But later I realize that the detour has led me into territory I would never have seen otherwise.

Life's detours can also be gifts, derailing our plans but leading us to trails we wouldn't have discovered any other way. Those diversions might also reveal God's surprises in ways we never expected.

Let me not grumble too insistently about the circumstances that force me to change plans!

51 | New Apostles

On the south coast of Australia you can find the Great Ocean Road. It runs along the edge where the force of the Southern Ocean meets the Australian land mass.

Eventually you will reach the famous Twelve Apostles—rock formations standing proudly along this coastal edge.

There never were twelve of them, and of those that ever existed, some have crumbled back into the ocean.

But notices there invite tourists to look out for signs of new apostles, as these are being formed all the time, even as the former ones crumble away.

The thought strikes home. Apostles walk the edge, just as Jesus did. And it is a continuous process, as each generation is called to discover its own place in the "apostolic succession."

Beyond Possibility | 52

THERE IS AN OLD ARABIC SAYING THAT THERE ARE two kinds of people: those who accept the horizon as the limit of possibility, and those who discover, as they journey, that there is always more to be discovered beyond every horizon.

I guess the difference lies in whether you are in a fixed position or still moving. For someone who has taken up a fixed position or attitude in a particular matter, there can be no more movement. Nothing further can be discovered. There is no room for debate and discussion because the subject is closed. There will be no more growth. If humanity as a whole had become fixed, we would not have moved beyond our prehistoric limitations.

But for the one who is open to possibilities not yet known or understood, the horizon of growth and learning is constantly beckoning the explorer beyond existing boundaries.

The closed person still lives on a "flat earth." The open-minded person lives in an ever-expanding mystery.

53 | One Step at a Time

It's a very dark night in a very remote village in the hills of northern England. There are no street lights and no stars. Just the very occasional glimmer of light from behind the curtains of scattered cottages.

The road is uneven and fraught with bends and potholes—really, a bit like the road of life. I try to discern the way ahead by training the meager beam of my flashlight into the middle distance. Its light is swallowed up immediately by the darkness and disappears into the night without adding in the slightest to my pathfinding.

I try a different tack. I shine the little light I have on the few feet of ground immediately ahead of me. The way opens up, step by step. No way of deciphering the mysteries that may lie ahead. Enough simply to trust the light, one step at a time.

Apostolic Succession | 54

ROYAL LINEAGES, APOSTOLIC SUCCESSIONS, AND the anointing that accompanies them—the various complex mechanisms we have established for the passing on of power and glory—all these are characterized by the laying-on of hands upon *heads*.

But God's touch on our lives, the touch that calls each of us to be a carrier and co-creator of God's Dream, happens when God's hand is laid upon our *hearts*.

It can be a very long journey from the head to the heart.

55 | The Ninety-Nine Acre Field

FOR A LAD WHO WAS GROWING UP ON A SMALL farmstead covering just forty-six acres in total, it was hard to imagine that a single field could be more than twice the size of his entire world. Yet for the old plowman, the ninety-nine-acre field was his daily workplace. It seemed to the boy to be farther than the eye could see in every direction; yet it was a field to be plowed, like his father's own fields, with a team of horses and a plow and a steady hand.

Now, with fifty years of hindsight, he still knows that a ninety-nine-acre field is a very big field to plow, just as he remembers the old plowman's wisdom on how to accomplish this task.

The first furrow has to be perfectly straight because it sets the course for every furrow after it. To achieve that perfect straightness, you had to look into the far distance, between the heads of the two horses, and fix your gaze on a landmark at the farther edge: a tree, a rock, or perhaps a cluster of bushes. The secret of the straight furrow was to keep your sights always focused on that chosen landmark and plough toward it. If you let your attention wander for long to the immediate surroundings, or to the horses or the plough in your hand, you would soon lose the focus, and the furrow would start to wander.

The fixed point on the horizon is the One who leads the Way—the One who makes the first perfectly straight furrow—the Way that follows the dream.

56 | The Dancing Leaf

It is a fine spring morning in a forest near Ottawa. The early flowers are just beginning to show themselves through the crust of still-wintry earth. As I stroll through the woods, I have no idea that, on the other side of the Atlantic, a lady I have yet to meet is feeling far from springlike. She had once been a liturgical dancer, but six years ago a new pastor at her parish church had decreed that there should be no dancing in church. She had been devastated, but had obediently tried to forget her dancing. Unknown to me, she is even now preparing to come on retreat in Scotland.

I wander along the winding pathway, stopping to admire the trilliums—flowers that don't grow in my own native land—and then I notice something strange. A leaf—dead, brown, and withered from last year's fall—is floating in the breeze, just at eye level. I stop to investigate, wondering why it doesn't either fly away or fall to the earth. Even on closer inspection I can't see any reason for its behavior. No sign of anything connecting it to the nearby tree. Nothing. An hour later I return by the same route, and there is the leaf again, still dancing in front of my eyes. This time I look more closely and find a thin, gossamer thread, barely visible, which is holding the leaf securely to a nearby branch. Mystery solved.

Yet, strangely, the incident of the dancing leaf keeps coming back to my mind. I find myself reflecting on the nature of that gossamer thread. If the leaf had not been connected by that thread it would certainly have flown off in the wind and eventually fallen to the ground. The connection was a vital one. If that thread had been a rod of steel, however, then the leaf would have remained connected, but it would not have danced.

A little while after this incident I am facilitating a retreat in Scotland, and I happen to tell the participants the story of the dancing leaf. On the last morning, we all gather in the little chapel to break bread together. After communion one of the retreatants feels moved to dance. We are spellbound. The beauty, the grace, and the power of her dance leaves us all speechless and deeply blessed. Afterward she shares the story of how six years earlier she had been asked to stop dancing; how she had resigned herself to never performing sacred dance again; how the thread that connected her to the vine had turned to steel, but how the story had released her joy in dance once more.

What threads connect us to one another? And are they liberating or paralyzing? The danger of a leash that is too short and a connection that is too rigid is as great as the danger of not being connected at all. Finding the balance between connection and control is a challenge, but we have a model of how to get it right. He is the one who knows that when you are truly connected to the source of your being, you can dance freely and joyfully into the future, even in the shadow of a cross.

Keeping Going

57

THE CATACLYSMIC ENDING OF WORLD WAR II HAS left a shattered Europe in its wake. From deep in the southeast of a devastated Germany, a twelve-year-old girl, homeless and orphaned, sets off on a long, long walk. In her pocket she fingers a slip of paper, on which is the address of a distant relative far away in the west of the country.

On her journey she meets every kind of hardship: fear, loneliness, and raw, aching hunger. What keeps her going? Just that little slip of paper.

What keeps me going when I can't see the rhyme or reason in things? What keeps me getting out of bed every morning and putting one foot in front of the other? What serves as my little slip of paper, convincing me that there is a real destination to walk toward?

I don't keep going because some system of authority says I should. That would never be enough to see me through the storms. I don't keep going because of the teaching I learn from books, even the most sacred of books. That teaching may be wise and true, but it wouldn't keep the flame flickering inside me through long dark nights.

I keep going because just once in a while, very occasionally, I have felt the touch of God on my heart. It's a bit like living under perpetual cloud cover and then going up in an aircraft, above the clouds, to where the sun is always shining. If you have glimpsed the sun just once, you know it is always there, the ultimate reality. If you have known even the lightest touch of God upon your life, you know that God is always there, the ultimate reality.

What you have once known, you can never *not* know. It will keep you going whatever happens. Cherish it in your heart, just as that little girl curled her cold fingers around her precious slip of paper.

Following

58

FOLLOWING THE RULES ONLY MAKES US OBEDIENT.
Following the Christlight makes us whole.

Following the rules can make us intolerant and self-righteous.
Following the Christlight makes us compassionate.

Following the rules can even make us dangerous.
Following the Christlight can put us at risk.

What will my epitaph say?
"She kept the rules, and here she lies," or
"She followed the dream, and God knows where she is now"?

SOUTH

Choosing Life

In a Native American story, a grandfather tells his grandson how in every human heart two wolves dwell and are in constant conflict with one another until the day we die. The little boy looks up and asks, "But Grandad, which wolf wins?" Grandad replies, "The one you feed!"

What we feed, by giving it our energy and attention, will grow. What we starve, by withholding our energy and attention, will shrink. Which aspects of ourselves would we like to grow, and which would we prefer were not so robust?

In everything we have a choice, especially in the attitudes we adopt toward our circumstances. And always, ultimately, the choice is between what tends to make us, other people, and all creation more fully alive, and what tends to diminish and deaden the best in us and in the world around us.

It's time to turn our faces to the south, to the beams of the midday sun. May the light of due south sharpen our vision, enlighten all our choices, and help us to keep choosing those actions and attitudes that make us more fully human, more completely alive.

Big Visions and Daily Details

59

It's graduation day. The new graduates from a large metropolitan medical school wait in line to climb the three steps to the dais to receive their diplomas before descending the three steps again to return to their seats. The dean exchanges a few words with each graduate—a simple question, such as, "Have you enjoyed your time here?" or "What are you planning to do next?"

Then he turns his attention to the parents and friends of the newly robed, and tells us how he has presided over several similar ceremonies that week. He recounts the reactions of two particular graduates to his not-too-searching question: "What are you going to do next?"

The first had responded, after a moment's thought, "I'm going to be a world-class brain surgeon." The dean had congratulated him on his graduation and wished him every success in his career. The second, a few hundred graduates farther down the line, had been asked the same question: "What are you going to do next?" She, too, had given the question several moments of thoughtful attention, before replying: "I'm going to turn left and walk very carefully down these three steps."

Both graduates are right. We are called to be active participants in a Big Dream, God's Dream that all of creation, under the power of love, will be fulfilled. But the way we make it a reality is by attending to the next three steps right in front of us. The big vision without the daily detail is merely daydreaming. The daily detail without the big dream can become just a toilsome trudge.

We honor the big vision when we keep in mind, with every step, that we are movers and players in a cosmic drama way beyond our imagination. We honor the daily detail every time we ask, in a specific situation, "What is the more loving, the more life-giving, the more Christlike thing to do next?"

Portable Weather | 60

I SMILE OVER A LIGHTHEARTED EXCHANGE BETWEEN two radio presenters on the car radio, as I drive through streaming rain, straining to focus on the road ahead through the hypnotic back-and-forth of the windshield wipers. One of them has just come back from his vacation and is delighted to report that he has enjoyed two weeks of sunshine in southern France. The other is just about to go away on holiday, and remarks ruefully that whenever he arranges his vacation and wherever he goes, it always seems to rain on him.

"In fact," he comments, "I have my own personal cloud that always travels with me." The vision of this little man roaming the world with his own little cloud always hovering above, ready to drench him, isn't quite as lighthearted as it sounds. I guess I know people like that. You can even see the shadow of their cloud upon their faces. They are always expecting the worst, and as a result they often get it. And then there are the folks who always seem to carry a bit of blue sky around with them. Not a tropical heaven, but just enough blue to let a gleam of sunlight through, to light up their faces, and to bring a break in the prevailing gloom for everyone they meet.

The great thing is, our portable weather isn't something that is imposed upon us. It's something we can choose.

The Great Divide | 61

There is a little kopje, or hillock, in the heart of Johannesburg. A raindrop falling upon this kopje will join the flow of water either into the Orange River, and hence to the South Atlantic, or into the Limpopo River, and hence into the Indian Ocean. This hillock is the boundary between two watersheds and marks the great divide between the flow of South Africa's waters, either east or west.

Of course if you are a raindrop, I guess it doesn't much matter which way you go, since all rivers eventually flow into an ocean, and all oceans are good news. It wouldn't make much difference, ultimately, to the destination, though it would make a huge difference to the *journey*, and the landscape and human situations through which you would pass.

But what about our own choices? Some of them switch the points on our life's journey and change its course forever. Some barely cause a ripple in our lives. But all of them make a difference. Some drops are quiet and small: We choose how to react to a call for help, or to some unwanted criticism; we choose a word of encouragement or disparagement, a kind or an angry gesture. And some of them are big and compelling: We choose where to invest our life's energy; we choose whether to resist or collude with injustice, and sometimes the choice is costly. Each drop, each choice, has power at a personal level, but it will also flow into bigger and bigger rivers—the rivers of our community choices, our national choices, and our global choices. Without the personal choices for peace and justice, there will be no peace or justice in our nations and our world. A choice that betrays a personal trust will also pollute the rivers of all human interaction.

Whether they appear to be important or slight, our choices are all raindrops that fall steadily upon the great divide of life, which separates what is life-giving from what is life-denying. In everything we do or say, or even think, we are weighing in, however slightly, either with the creative or with the destructive movements that are shaping the future of humanity. Every self-focused choice—for retaliation over reconciliation, for the benefit of *me* or *my group* over the needs of all creation—makes us *all* less human, and impedes the fulfilling of God's Dream for humanity. Every choice that adds to the store of love, hope, and trust in the world is a choice for the ocean of God's love.

In every choice we make, we stand astride this Great Divide. It matters, which way each raindrop chooses to flow. Every raindrop either nourishes or harms the future. Every choice decides.

62 | Responding to the Stranger

A FRIEND OF MINE IS A BUSY ACADEMIC AND ACTIVIST for peace and justice. He has received an e-mail from a student—a complete stranger—that asks a searching question. He knows he must either respond comprehensively or brush her off with a courteous apology. He really doesn't have time for random enquiries from obscure students.

He reflects and decides to sit down and provide the thoughtful response that the question merits.

Three weeks later he receives a letter from a professor at a respected university. The writer thanks him for taking the trouble to answer the student's question so thoroughly—a question he had asked her to send on his behalf. He invites my friend to participate in an important new project. They will become colleagues and co-workers in the cause of justice because a question from an unknown enquirer was handled with respect.

"Oft goes the Christ in stranger's guise."

Unexpected Moments of Independent Thought | 63

THE MULE HANDLER IN THE GRAND CANYON warns would-be riders that mules are occasionally inclined to "unexpected moments of independent thought."

Good for them! Maybe they will get enough such moments to decide whether or not they actually *want* to trek down into the canyon every day in the blistering heat with tourists on their backs.

On the other hand, they might use their independence to take themselves and their riders off in dangerous directions.

I get moments of independent thought too, occasionally. I guess I need to think carefully about what I do with them. Some of them may lead me to new heights of creativity or generosity. Others may mis-lead me to insist on stubbornly following my own will, regardless of the consequences.

64 | The Enemy Within

We are enjoying a meal, and the window is open. The summer streams into the room, and so do the flies and the wasps.

My attention is focused on the aggressive wasps that might sting me.

My companion is more concerned about the apparently harmless flies settling on the butter and possibly carrying unseen diseases.

It makes me think about the hazards of living. What is worse, I ask myself—the things that buzz and sting and hurt in an obvious way, or the things that look harmless but carry silent, secret poison?

Do I spend too much effort fending off possible aggressors, while less visible dangers go unattended?

Jesus said to the Pharisees: "From the outside you look upright, but inside you are full of hypocrisy and lawlessness." I think he would prefer that I think less about the wasps and more about the flies. Less about the imagined enemies waiting to attack us from outside and more about the subtle toxins polluting us from within.

Diamonds and Dewdrops | 65

THE MORNING DEW, SPARKLING ON THE GRASS, reflects all the colors of the rainbow. Each dewdrop has become a diamond.

I'm thinking of a diamond ring I cherished, but which was recently stolen. My heart saddens under the weight of the thought.

But then a question takes shape in my heart, one that seems to come from God:

"Which would you rather be? A diamond, worth a thousand dollars, that can so easily be lost or stolen? Or a dewdrop that will have evaporated by noon, but will have soaked into the earth and nourished new life in the process?"

Diamonds are hard and solid. Dewdrops are so fleeting. Diamonds bring wealth. Dewdrops bring life.

My heart knows that I will choose the dewdrop.

66 | Don't Melt the Angel

There's a lot of anger around right now. In fact I feel as though I'm inwardly boiling. Mainly around hurtful attitudes and events in the church.

A friend, who can't possibly know what's churning around inside me, gives me a little angel made of beeswax.

It calms me down a bit, and eventually my angel has a word in my ear: "Take care that the heat of your anger doesn't melt me."

It makes me stop and think. There is a heat that heals—the heat of passion for justice and truth.

And there is a heat that hurts, because it is so intense and unyielding.

The one refines my experience into gold. The other melts my angels.

I pray to learn to distinguish between the two.

Event Horizons | 67

Events happen to me. They evoke responses. They shape my course, sometimes for better, sometimes for worse.

But I easily forget that *I* am an event that happens to others. Am I an event that evokes the best in them or one that provokes the worst? When my path crosses the path of another person, whether in a casual or a deliberate way, what difference will that encounter make to the other person's life?

Do my interactions and relationships with others leave them closer to who they truly are or farther away?

Does my presence deepen others' life in God, or undermine it? Am I using them to build up my own kingdom, or relating to them in a way that nourishes God's Kingdom for all?

68 | The Importance of Not Being Necessary

I STRETCH OUT ON THE SOFA AT THE END OF THE day, to relax and listen to some music. My cat comes immediately and lies down across my chest, purring deeply.

The moment brings to mind the German word for livestock, *Nutztier* (literally, "an animal we can use") and it strikes me with delight that my pet cat is definitely an "Unnutztier"—useless in the best possible way—unnecessary but indispensable.

Perhaps in his own way my cat is showing me something about my relationships with creation and with other people. Is my attitude ever *How can I use this person to further my own desires?* What a difference when I am simply in relationship with others because of pure delight in them and in their otherness.

I go back, deeply contented, to attend to the music and the purring.

The Ocean of Memory | 69

It's a magnificent May morning—England at her finest. I find myself on a sunny spot, in a cliff-side garden, on the south coast. At my feet the English Channel is lapping gently. Once, in what seems like a previous existence, I walked these cliffs as a child, holding my parents' hands. Once, on these sands, I made sandcastles and watched the ocean wash them away with every new tide.

This part of the coast is populated mainly by retired folk. I passed many of the retirement complexes on my way here and am on the way to visit an old friend who retired here years ago.

As I walk these leafy lanes, I imagine that I am floating through an ocean of memories. So many of the people here are living from their memories. I see elderly gentlemen in their summer shirts, on solitary strolls, perhaps remembering how it used to be when their wives walked with them. I watch senior ladies dreaming their dreams on park benches. Their bones and flesh are here, but where are their minds and hearts?

The thing about this ocean of memory is that for some people it is buoyant and alive; it is what holds them up and keeps them going, especially when skies are gray. But for others that same ocean of memories is what sucks them into the depths of disappointment and regret.

Same ocean. Very different effects.

Perhaps we each have a choice about how we relate to the mountain of memories upon which our life's "today" is perched. Will we choose to let those memories strengthen and uphold us? Or will we let them drag us down until we become the prisoners of our past?

Everyone I meet on this cliff path would have a different response I guess. But *my* response is my responsibility, my choice.

The Special Race | 70

A colleague sends me a report he has seen on the Internet about an incident at a school Sports Day. The school served both "normal" children and those who were physically or intellectually challenged. As far as possible the education of all the children was integrated, but when it came to Sports Day, to give the disadvantaged children a fair chance, they were competing only against each other in their own race. At least that was what their teachers had planned.

The mainstream races and competitions were completed, the little ribbons for first, second, and third place awarded amid enthusiastic applause from proud parents. Then came the time for the race for the children with special needs. They all lined up at the starting line. The starter pistol sounded, and off they went. All went well, as their friends and parents cheered them on. Then, in midrace, one of the children stumbled and fell. Every single child in the race stopped running and turned back to help the fallen friend.

After a moment of stunned silence, while the children helped their friend to find his feet again, a storm of spontaneous applause broke out from the onlookers. The "normal" children had shown them the meaning of success. These special children had shown them what it means to choose life, even if that means relinquishing the hope of success.

The Peace Vote

71

During the Second World War, there were a few hundred powerful men who directed hostilities and made choices that would cause maximum destruction to their enemies.

There were hundreds of thousands of men, women, and children who, waking to the aftermath of those acts of destruction, made the choice to get up, go out, bury the dead, bind the wounded, and rebuild their homes.

In the twenty-first century there are a few hundred politicians making strategies of war.

There are millions of ordinary people making plans for peace.

Living as though war were inevitable makes war inevitable.

Living as if peace were possible, makes peace possible.

72 | The Funny Scales

IT'S DEFINITELY TIME TO FIX MY LITTLE PATCH OF front garden. It is going completely wild with lavender that is threatening to take over the street. Much as I love the scent as I climb over the vine into my front door, I decide to bring my little patch into line with my neighbor's, and lay some ornamental gravel instead, with more manageable pots of flowering plants.

You wouldn't believe how heavy gravel bags are until you try to hoist them into the trunk of the car. The first thing I do is put my back out in the effort. A kindly neighbor sees my plight and offers to collect my fourteen bags of gravel from the garden center in his truck. My back says Alleluia.

The next thing I do is put my eye out, in a close encounter with a recalcitrant lavender bush. The following morning I look in the mirror and see one eye beautifully white with a blue iris, and the other an angry blood red with a blue iris. I look like something out of a Frankenstein movie, but fortunately no permanent harm done. The garden is fighting back.

And finally (I hope, finally!) I put my nose out of joint by bashing it with the rake.

Time to sit down with a cup of tea. I e-mail my crazy friend in the Bronx and can almost hear her peals of laughter as she reads about my adventures with the lavender. She later phones me to sympathize, and doesn't help by commenting that my red eye and blue iris might turn to a nice shade of lavender, like Liz Taylor's eyes. I mention politely that it was lavender that started the whole thing in the first place. But, sitting there, enjoying my tea, I know I am at a pivotal moment in the day. I will either cry over all my trials or I will howl with laughter over my own stupidity.

I can see the moment of choice so clearly, like a set of kitchen scales. On the one side are the worry weights. Will my eye recover? Will my nose go black? On the other side are the funny weights. How do I keep a straight face when I tell people that my eye has become so deranged because I put a stick in it, and my nose is flat because it fell out with the rake?

I choose to err on the funny side of life. It might not change the outcome, but it sure makes me feel better. What's more, when I laugh the world laughs with me. When I worry, I worry alone.

73 | Breaking Free

A Ugandan friend is recalling his childhood in a very poor rural community where the people survived by eating wild birds. He remembers one bird in particular, a small bird with beautiful yellow plumage. The villagers set traps for these birds, and often when they went to collect the catch, they would find not a yellow bird, but only a fractured, twisted leg. The bird desired its freedom so much that it would break off its own leg in order to fly free.

How much would I be willing to pay for my freedom?

If I sense that something is holding me captive—the weight of circumstance, or another person's dominance, or my own crippling memories or negative attitudes—how high a price am I prepared to pay for the freedom I am called to as a child of God? Do I have the courage of the little yellow bird? Can I sever myself from the captivity of the lesser life to be free for the grace of the abundant life that God holds out to me?

SOUTHWEST

Breaking Down

LIGHT WANES, SHADOWS LENGTHEN, THE DAY HAS passed its zenith. We look back over our lives, and we know the ache of regret, the sting of remorse. Some of the dreams we dreamed now lie in broken fragments. The evidence of death is not hard to find. The obstacles that impede our way forward wait around every corner. Prayer can stall, and questions rob us of our once-clear certainties. When the setting sun casts its glow over our achievements, we see only weakness and helplessness: arthritic bones, dark nights, empty dereliction, and impotence in the face of tragedy.

But a clump of clover grows amid the desolation. The storm churns up new nutrients from the ocean bed. God lives in our empty spaces, where there is nothing left to block the flow of divine love.

Our faith rests on a moment of apparently total breakdown on Calvary. Let us acknowledge the necessity of that breakdown in our own lives and the lives of our societies, systems, and institutions. Let us not strive to avoid it. It is the paschal mystery, and it asks of us just one thing: "Trust me."

In Sickness and in Health | 74

A RABBIT SITS IN THE MIDDLE OF THE PATH. I expect him to run away as I approach. Instead he just hobbles into the undergrowth and watches me pass. For a moment our eyes meet. I try to communicate to him that I mean no harm. Maybe he acknowledges it, in some mute way that only our souls understand.

He is a sick bunny. It is only his weakness and his vulnerability that keep him grounded in my vicinity. Only his weakness and vulnerability that make possible this moment of connection between us, however fear-filled on his part.

A few minutes later I am nearly bowled over by a healthy specimen, who shoots out from the bushes and runs off ahead of me in terror. No chance of any conversations there.

It leaves me wondering where my own deepest desires really lie. Do I choose autonomy, security, and two strong legs to flee with—or vulnerability, risk, and two clear eyes to see with?

If my longing is really for intimacy with God, and with others, however fleeting and fear-filled, then maybe I, too, will find my heart's desire only when my weakness grounds me.

When the Barriers Are Down

75

The gates to the railway crossing are down again this morning. Why does it seem that those gates are always closed when I am waiting to use the road?

Yet I have to smile when I remember how often I stand on the platform at the railway station, wondering how long it will be before the train arrives. I'm happy to see the gates go down then, because I know that means the train is approaching.

Strange, how those things that open the gates for some of us are closing them for others, and what closes the gates for us in some situations opens them in others.

Jesus warned us not to pull up the good plants along with the weeds, but to let both grow together. Perhaps our fleeting fortunes and misfortunes, our temporary advantages and inconveniences, are a bit like that. Patience allows them to be what they are, and eventually reveals the grace in each of them.

76 | Disarming Power

MY OLD FRIEND CAN HARDLY MOVE HER FINGERS because of crippling arthritis. She says she feels useless and powerless.

But she makes the most exquisite pastry. The pastry turns out so well because she has no choice but to handle it with the lightest touch.

A more forceful cook could never produce such light and delicate pastry.

Maybe true power really does flow more readily through human weakness than through human strength. Maybe a disarming smile can achieve more than an armed intervention.

A Stopped Clock | 77

My prayer stalls. My spiritual journey seems to be at a standstill.

I glance up at a clock in the street: Twenty past two. Surely it was showing that time this morning when I looked. And yesterday . . .

And I recall my father's wisdom. He used to say, "Even a stopped clock is right twice a day"—unlike a clock that is running fast, or slow, which is *never* right.

Somehow I feel better about the stopped state of my journey with God. Better, maybe, than running ahead under my own steam, or dragging back in my resistance.

Maybe, for now, I will just be a stopped clock and leave any necessary adjustments to the clockmaker.

78 | Tunnel Vision

THE WINDING COASTAL ROAD SUDDENLY LURCHES into a tunnel. I feel irrationally apprehensive. Vision gone. Car lights on. Don't switch lanes. Don't overtake. Go carefully.

Whatever happened to the soaring hillsides and the dappling sea along this scenic Welsh coast?

Reception fails on the car radio. Just crackling and static. Cut off. Incommunicado.

I am familiar with times such as these on my interior journey. Still, they always take me by surprise. They make me feel a bit fearful—even resentful that the consolations are cut off when I need them most.

Then some good spirit taps gently on the walls of my brain. "The tunnel is bringing you through terrain you couldn't cross in any other way."

Who knows what dark nights of the soul are good for, but I'm just going to have to believe that God knows the reasons and the results, and that the God who doesn't offer ways around life's obstacles is always alongside me, on the way through.

Power Failure

79

I DON'T WANT TO GO ON.
I just want empty space.
No words.
No thinking.
No prayer.
No-thing.
No-body.

At the station, crowds mill around the platform, watching the indicators. Something is wrong again. It's 8:15 and I see that the 7:33 hasn't gone yet. The 8:27 isn't even on the screen. I ask what's happening.

The station attendant tells me there is a general power failure and nothing is moving, in or out.

Total immobility now.
Total chaos later.
I know exactly how it feels.
I have a general power failure of my own.

I come home instead.

Home into the hope of empty space.

Home, instead, into a barrage of phone calls, tears, phone calls.

Mass at 1 p.m.

Five communicants, and the chaplain has filled the chalice too full.

The chalice is too full, Lord.

Are you listening?

Gravity Revisited | 80

In God's realm, the law of gravity seems to operate in the opposite direction. Our moments of helplessness are the weightless, empty pockets of ourselves that sink back into God's center, and our moments of power, real or imagined, take us off somewhere at a tangent, out into the distant regions of our inner universe.

That's why it's possible to be thankful, with hindsight, for the empty spaces that have drawn us closer to home, and it is needful to ask forgiveness for the heavy lumps of power that threaten to carry us off into outer space.

81 | The Gift of Deficiency

The Samaritan woman at the well would never have met Jesus if she'd had a water supply at home.

It is in what we lack that we are most open to all we can become.

Why do we bombard God with our prayers for what we lack to be provided? Perhaps we should be asking God not to supply our wants, but to dwell within them.

Partners for Life | 82

THE SWEETEST WINE IS PRESSED FROM THE GRAPES that have been left on the vine the longest, particularly those that have endured the rigors of the frost.

Honey comes from the creatures that can fatally sting us.

The lighthouse stands on the most exposed and dangerous rocks.

The healing powers of radiation were discovered by a woman who was killed by them.

Destruction and creation are inseparable partners in the project of life.

83 | Vacant Possession

GOD LOVES EMPTINESS! THIS IS IRONIC, IN VIEW OF our constant attempts to fill up God with praise and offerings and our many Kingdom projects. The winter season especially provides vivid reminders of God's preference for emptiness and poverty. The trees are bare, bereft of their October glory. The holiday cottages are empty, and the "Vacancies" boards are evident everywhere. Even the sun has withdrawn to just a few hours' appearance each day. Growth has gone underground for the winter, to the invisible realm where transformation happens.

Yet vacancy is the very thing God is looking for, in God's continuing journey to Bethlehem in search of a place to be born. Our fullness, real or imagined, is of no more use to God than the overflowing inn with no space left in which Christ could be born. Our well-ordered lives and carefully constructed systems are found, in the end, to be incapable of receiving the seed of eternity. Instead, God seeks out the sheds and the stables and the neglected outhouses of our lives, and lies down right there in the mud and the mess and the muddle of our living, to call us into the labor of love that will, in the fullness of time, give birth to all that we can become.

There are two problems with this plan. First, we will do almost anything to cover up the mess and the muddle, and to fill up the emptiness within us. And second, we are extremely unwilling to wait for "the fullness of time." Sometimes I wonder what would happen if, when it came time to sow our seeds in spring, or plant our potatoes, we refused to do so because of all the dirt involved, or if, as the seeds and tubers began to grow, we would dig them up because they were taking too long. Patience doesn't come very high on any list of human—especially Western—values.

God thinks otherwise. God actively *chooses* our empty holes and grime-encrusted corners for the beginnings of a new birth in our hearts. And God waits for as long as it takes for our growing and ripening, all the while tending that growth with personal love and care. All that is asked of us is our "Yes! Let it be done in me as you dream it shall be."

I seriously need to ask for the grace to look with God's eyes a little more deeply into the places within that I would rather cover over, and to open the empty, aching spaces inside me to the God who desires to plant the seed of Life precisely *there*.

Bees among the Clover | 84

I WONDER WHY I HAVE NEVER NOTICED THIS CLOVER before. Today the brilliance of its full pink flowers leaps out to greet me and I almost want to apologize for the countless times I must have walked past without noticing. It is just a corner of derelict land squeezed between the train station, highway, and the desolate side street that leads to my place of work.

A building must have stood here once, because this land is strewn with broken bricks and lumps of concrete and rotting plaster. Perhaps, a home stood here, years ago. People lived and died, worked and laughed and struggled here and left a pile of rubble when they moved on. That must have been years ago, because the rough grass has taken hold of the sharp edges, and the groundsel and chickweed entangle their yellowness with the deep pensive pinks of the clover.

Times of dereliction scar most lives, and sometimes it seems that we are lying on a bed of rubble, where the familiar structures of denial and defense have been demolished and crumbled into dust—and where something new might be seeded and take root.

Today an early bee hovers over the clover. There will be sweetness out of destruction. It might take years, but there will be sweetness.

A Course in Midwifery | 85

It always intrigues me that the English and the German words describing the time when a woman is preparing to give birth are so apparently opposite in meaning.

The English word, *confinement*, suggests an experience of being closed into a small space, being imprisoned, limited, constrained. At its best it hints of loving care that the patient receives passively. At its worst it threatens us with hospital routines and institutionalization.

The German word *Entbindung* reminds us of what this time is really about—"unbinding," releasing, letting go, unfurling, revealing a mystery hitherto hidden from our sight, setting a new human being free to become who she is destined to be.

The universe has done this for us. The violent death of a supernova has set free the elements that now shape our solar system and our earthly being. Time and weather have unbound the canyons. Cataclysmic upheavals have released the oceans and mountains. Waves of labor pain have launched each one of us into life as embodied human souls.

What will we do with the vision of Jesus of Nazareth? Will we confine it to a box of our own making and limit it to the dimensions of our understanding? Or will we give it the space to unfurl and reveal itself in a world where there is no safety but everything to discover?

Are we searching for a system of salvation in which to settle, or a process of discovery that will always take us beyond our self-imposed limits? Will we permit the disintegration of our small certainties in order to give birth to a mystery that transcends all understanding? Dare we acknowledge that every birth is accompanied by anguish and breakdown, and that we are called to be midwives to one another's arrival to this life?

Desolation | 86

THERE ARE DAYS IN THE DEPTH OF WINTER when Ashburys station in the poorest district of Manchester in northern England seems like a place that had fallen off the edge of the universe. Today I am alone again on the platform. The ticket office is closed and barred for fear of vandalism. The tracks look as though there may never be another train, however long I wait. An icy wind bites through the damp January air.

I walk up and down the deserted platform, trying to keep warm. In the distance a cold cityscape rises in steely silhouette. There is no hint of humanity in its shape—it looks surreal and menacing, rising into the low, brooding black clouds.

There are three sets of train signals, all resolutely red. Immovably, unyieldingly red. This is a no-go area and I feel suddenly, irrationally threatened.

The station becomes a locked space, in spite of the cold winds that pass through it and the living damp that inhabits it. I wouldn't know if there really were no trains at all on this railway route. Such things happen, and communications fail without our knowing either cause or remedy. I wonder how long I would wait in vain for release from this imprisoning waste, before giving up and seeking other solutions. Then I wonder about those for whom such wastes are home, whose lives are lived on the margins of that sinister skyline and are forever bounded by signals to stop.

Eventually, when time seems to have stopped its aching passage, along with all activity on the rails, one of the red lights changes to yellow. As always, I'm surprised that my heart should feel a little thrill at this subtle change in the landscape of desolation. It means that there is life somewhere. I wait another few minutes, eagerly gazing at the signals, still pacing the platform as if my activity might bring about the arrival of a train.

At last, a train's headlight looms up out of the murkiness. It's going far too fast. It isn't going to stop. I step back as the train glides scornfully past the narrow platform. The lights change back to red, with a ripple of mocking laughter. Will my light ever be green? The unspoken prayer, which is about much more than a suburban rail connection, is quietly strangled inside me.

I turn away with a shiver, seeking shelter against a grimy wall, numbed with the cold and hardly caring any more. There is a low rumbling sound, slowing to a standstill. I breathe out my relief and board the train. I'm on the network again. I'm going somewhere.

87 | Seeds of the Storm

A TYPHOON HITS THE PACIFIC OCEAN. EVERYTHING runs for cover, especially human beings in boats. Nothing is spared the storm's ferocity.

The turtle knows about typhoons. She dives deep and stays low for as many hours as she can without surfacing for breath. Meanwhile all hell breaks loose.

She waits.

She knows that the storm that throws everything into chaos ultimately brings life. It stirs up the waters and causes fresh nutrients to be released. When the storm subsides, there will be fresh life and new beginnings.

Dying to Live

88

AN OLD FRIEND IS DYING. ALL HIS CHILDREN AND grandchildren are gathered at his bedside. My friend long ago decided to refuse resuscitation when the end approached and to spend his final hours in dignity, surrounded by those he loves, rather than in the clinical twilight world of the life support machine.

As the family accompany him to this threshold, they recall the stories of who he has been and of what he has meant to them. If there have been mistakes and failures, as there are in everybody's story, these are not emphasized, but passed over in loving forgiveness. They remember the countless ways in which their father and grandfather brought something unique and special to this world. Beneath and beyond their sorrow at this time of leave-taking there is also joy and thanksgiving, even celebration. For harvest time is here, and though the darkness falls, the fruits of this passing life will remain to nurture the ones who remain.

In a sense, the children and grandchildren are gathered here to receive their legacy. It's not a monetary legacy, nor a legacy that might provoke conflict and jealousy. The legacy they receive is for all of them. His dying brings them closer. This man, whom they love, has become an intimate part of each one of them. He leaves behind not only his DNA, but his spiritual bequest. He held their hands as they first learned to walk. He guided their hearts and souls into paths of integrity and truth. They came into the world with nothing. He leaves them with bountiful spiritual riches they can repay only by passing them on to those who will follow after.

Artificial life support would have blocked this rich exchange.

Today, so many of our familiar structures and ways of doing things are dying, especially, perhaps, in our religious traditions. Yet at the heart of our Christian tradition there is a death. Only through this death can there be a resurrection, a breakthrough to transcendence. If we have the courage and honesty to face this dying and to gather and celebrate all that these things have meant to us, to receive the legacy of all that they have become in us, then we shall be ready to embrace the next chapter of our sacred story. If we remain in denial, and put the patient on life support, we will miss the point. We will be denying Calvary, and blocking resurrection.

New life is always preceded by a dying. It was true of the stars and galaxies, and it is true for our systems and institutions. The gap between the dying and the transcending is terrifying. That is why Jesus walked it before us—and walks it with us. This dying asks of us that we cross the bridge of trust, letting go of the past with love, and reaching out in hope to all that calls us forward.

89 | Soul Soil

In my soul there is a story,
of a child's first sense of the divine,
of early bruising from collisions with walls of opposition,
and struggles to discover my life's authentic course.

A story that knows the aching and aloneness
left behind by the death of hope-begun relationships
and dried-up residues of long-forgotten fragrances
and pangs of sorrow for miscarried joys.

The story is the graveyard of the past and the soil of all that shall be.
In the soil grow the seeds that my past has planted,
nourished by the ashes of experience
watered by my tears,
and germinated by the sunlight of unexpected grace.

There is greening in the soil.
There is gold in the story.

WEST

Breaking Through

I SHARE WITH A WISE FRIEND MY CONFUSION OF feelings following a traumatic life event: anger, resentment, and grief, all mixed up with relief and even of liberation; feelings of wanting to extend a reconciling hand and wanting to rant and rage. My friend listens, then responds with guidance that takes me totally by surprise.

"Nurse your resentment," he suggests. "Hold it carefully in your heart like a candle flame. Let it burn as long as it needs. Then, only when you are ready to do so, blow it out."

We turn to the west now, and watch the sun slip over the horizon, leaving us in the night. Is it the end of something, or the beginning? When I am finally ready to blow out the flame of the resentments I am nursing, will I be left in darkness, or will I find a new light deep within, capable of leading me to where I never thought to go?

The gentle light of resurrection beckons. It is the light of eternity, and it was always there, but we don't usually see it until we have traveled in the dark.

Expelled from Eden? | 90

A few times in my life, I have felt painfully excluded, or even expelled, from a place that had special meaning for me.

I guess I first felt this kind of pain—no, it was more like anger actually—when I was visiting the shrine of a saint who has long been a guiding mentor for my inner journey. I had traveled hundreds of miles to be there. I had spent the morning there in prayer. Then, as the clock ticked toward noon, the priests of the order that owned the shrine began to file in for their daily Eucharist. My heart soared briefly—and then sank abruptly as one of them came up to me and signaled in no uncertain terms that I should leave the chapel. I was not welcome. I was not one of them. I was to go.

I left, feeling expelled, rejected. I was furious. However, in order to expedite my leaving, the offending priest directed me toward the back exit from the place, which meant that in fact I had the time and the opportunity to walk quietly and alone through the private rooms that the saint had once inhabited. It even felt as if the saint himself was there with me, encouraging me to find new life in what seemed like sudden death.

Other forced leave-takings erupted in my life as the years moved on. In each case, when I looked back, I could see how the pain of those times eventually gave way to new ways of seeing things, new courage to live in new ways and even in new places, courage to question old assumptions and to become a searcher rather than one who has arrived.

Then one day a thought turned up in my mind and sat there with such a decisive clarity that I had to listen to it. "You once expelled your own child from your own body," it said. "Was *that* a rejection?" "Of course it wasn't. It was a birthing," I answered myself. "So might it not be that these other expulsions and rejections that you are nursing might also have been birthings?"

Well, the answer was obvious. Now I can feel gratitude for those times when people, or circumstances, shifted me so forcibly out of my comfort zone. Like a baby who goes too far over term, something in me would have died if I hadn't been forced through the birth canal. Now, years later, I can rejoice in the life that arose from the violent interruptions to my cozy settledness.

Blessed Forgetting | 91

RALPH HAD A MAJOR AND SUSTAINED DISAGREEMENT with his only daughter. There was no contact between them for years. She tried, but he wasn't letting go of a single one of the old resentments and grudges.

Then he had a stroke and lost most of his short- and medium-term memory. The grudges and resentments, and the reasons for them, were erased. He became, once more, open to his daughter's desire for healing and reconciliation.

Sometimes the angel of light flies on the shoulders of what appears to be the angel of darkness.

Sometimes grace flows in mysterious ways.

92 | Emptying, *Full*-filling

The miracle of Cana, of water turned to wine, would never have been discovered if the wine had not been poured out by the ones who had no reason to believe that it was anything but water, but did as Jesus told them.

Can I risk an outpouring of love, based on such a fragile thing as faith?

Being emptied is the last thing I want to happen. But it might be the first step toward transformation.

Stony Ground | 93

The finest grapes grow in France's Cognac region. Why is this terrain so special? Two reasons: the clarity of light and the unyielding harshness of the stony ground.

The vines strive up toward the clear light above them and strike deep strong roots to take hold in the hostile ground below them. The result is a strong, true, fruitful plant.

What makes me strive toward the light beyond me? And are the stones in my life's soil actually making me stronger? And when I am feeling bruised and broken, could the crushing be the means to something fine and beautiful?

94 | Sacred Scars

I PUT MY HAND IN THE OVEN A FEW WEEKS AGO AND scorched myself on the heating element. In normal times this would have been just a careless mistake for which my skin paid the penalty. But the times were not normal. I was in a dark space, following the breakdown of a significant relationship, and so this accident became an *incident*, which, in hindsight, has taken on something of the power of parable.

My close encounter with the grill left me, initially, quite oblivious of the pain that was about to follow. As is so often the case in these matters, the pain of trauma is delayed. The initial shock of what has happened simply doesn't sink in. There is a brief respite of stunned numbness before our minds and hearts must begin to deal with the fallout.

Needless to say, my hand soon registered its displeasure at being so undeservedly barbecued. For a while the wound screamed through my consciousness, allowing me to think of little else, yet refusing to allow itself to be touched with any kind of balm. The burn across my hand grew more livid with each day and left me helpless either to help myself or accept anyone else's help. My more personal trauma was behaving in much the same way: taking over every waking thought and every restless dream, yet, like a wounded animal, repelling any attempts at tender ministration.

Within a few days the pain began to subside. It was possible to touch the wound, and to apply soothing cream. I watched, not without a sense of wonder, how my body's self-healing capabilities began to work. The angry redness faded to a more conciliatory dark pink. The pain became less insistent. The scorched skin gradually fell away, and I could see this miraculous process taking place before my eyes, as a new skin cover began to form. Everything that had been damaged and destroyed was being gently set aside, health was being restored, and new tissue was being woven. The pain was still there, but it no longer dominated my mind. I was beginning to focus on the healing process instead, and even to cooperate with it.

The healing of an aching heart and devastated emotional life takes a lot longer than that; maybe it takes a lifetime. But my hand seemed to be telling me that healing is the real thing, and that Dame Julian of Norwich got it right when she said that "all *shall* be well." My hand is teaching my heart to trust the mystery that is ceaselessly striving for our greater good.

Day by day my skin has knitted back together, and now all I have left to show for my destructive adventure is a slight scar. I'm actually hoping that the scar never fades completely, because it is something of an icon for me. It leads me through and beyond itself to the place where I meet the Healer. It will always remind me that whatever the trauma, the permanent reality in which I live and move and have my being is about wholeness, not harm.

Our scars are our reminders, not just that we have been hurt but, more important, that we have been healed.

Wounded Blessings | 95

THERE IS A CUSTOM AMONG SOME NATIVE AMERICAN peoples, that when someone is bereaved or suffers any kind of traumatic loss, that person is invited to go out into the forest, carrying an axe. He or she chooses a tree to represent the loss or breakdown. Once the tree has been selected, the bereaved one (for every kind of loss in life is a bereavement) strikes several sharp blows into the bark of the tree. The wounds of the heart are inflicted, both symbolically and actually, upon the tree.

The tree is wounded, but not destroyed, and from then on the one who has suffered the loss is encouraged to visit the tree regularly, and to be present to its gradual healing, over time, from the wounds it has suffered. In this way, the tree and the mourner become one in their pain and in their healing until eventually what they share has become a deep and sacred scar.

96 | Touching the Tears

A YOUNG NURSE SIGNS ON FOR DUTY IN A MANHATTAN hospital. As she comes up from the subway, she is just in time to witness the impact of the second plane. She realizes that whatever is happening, it is going to demand all of her skills. So she rushes to her workplace and begins to minister to the injured and the dying, as ash falls from the skies, shrouding Manhattan in a blanket of death.

As a neurological specialist, it is her task to assess whether a casualty has suffered head trauma or is only in shock. It's not always an easy judgment. A young black patient is in front of her, a man in his twenties. He makes no response to any of her questions. It is impossible to tell whether there is brain damage. She focuses on his eyes. She catches the slightest glimmer of response through these windows of his soul, into his shattered yet sacred inner space. As their gazes meet for a moment, a tear slowly rises in each of his eyes, like the source of some deep and sorrowing river. Each tear flows oh so slowly down his cheeks, making two shining black rivers through the layer of ash that covers his skin.

At this point, the nurse has nothing more to say. For a moment she hesitates, and then she reaches out and gently, reverently, touches the tears.

It is a moment out of time—a moment that only God could have given. Something is released inside the heart of a broken man. He begins to speak. He pours out his story: He had been in the office with a colleague; he was able to fling himself under the desk, but his colleague had not been able to do so; he had watched his colleague die. . . . The nurse listens. All she can do is stay there, in her own helplessness.

When the world appears to be collapsing around you, and the landscape of your life is covered with ash, staying with the helplessness is really the only option. But that's the hardest thing! We want to have life under control. If circumstances seize that control away from us, we fight tooth and nail to regain it.

And then the moment comes when there is nothing to be done. When the screams subside and there is nothing left except the silence of shock. Then we finally come face to face with our helplessness. And it is only then that the miracle happens. In the face of nothing left to say, the nurse obeys some deep intuition that prompts her to reach out in a gesture of empathy and solidarity, and as soon as she does so, a cleansing and cathartic process is begun in her patient.

On the raw edges of human life, God reveals, to those who dare to look, the Calvary truth that out of brokenness a radically new wholeness can grow.

Lightning Strike | 97

A Native American word *shiwana* describes a healer who has been given his or her power by being struck by lightning.

First Nations people in Canada sometimes refer to seams of gold in the earth as "broken lightning."

Sometimes lightning strikes deep into our comfort zones and explodes our certainties.

And then? Just possibly our vulnerability carves out channels through which new life, and healing, grace, and power, might flow for others. Just possibly, seams of gold will appear.

98 | Hatched?

There's a tiny broken shell lying on the grass—a sky-blue, beautifully speckled shell.

My heart sinks as I stop to pick it up, thinking of one little chick whose journey into life was aborted by the untimely fall of its shell from the nest.

But why so sad, my heart? Why do I assume that the breaking was untimely? It's April, and the woodland is alive with birdsong. It's much more likely that this shell is the remains of a hatching, and the little chick may even now be perched on some high branch, looking down on me.

Perhaps the brokenness in my own life is not so much the monument to what might have been, but the sign of everything that is becoming. Perhaps some of my dreams are, after all, not broken, but hatched.

Sunken Treasure | 99

It just may be that, in the shipwrecks of your life, at the bottom of the ocean where your dreams are drowned, there is gold.

It just may be that, when the worst happens, you find out who you really are.

It just may be that in the deepest darkness, a new direction reveals itself, like the polestar in a black sky.

100 | Spending Power

I AM RIDICULOUSLY ELATED. I HAVE WON A PRIZE FOR the Idea of the Week at my place of work. A voucher for $50 has come to me out of the blue, to buy whatever book or books I choose.

I am in heaven. My elation seems to be out of proportion to the event, if I think about it rationally, but the sense of disproportion in no way detracts from the high I feel. I bounce home like a giddy teenager.

A week later I still haven't spent my prize. I ask myself why. As long as I have the $50 in my pocket, everything is possible. The whole world—at least the world of literature—lies potentially within reach. I can think of any book in the store, and it could be mine. I could even order a book that isn't in the store, and it could be mine.

It could be, but it won't be, unless I decide to change the potential into actual.

Perhaps this is what *incarnation* means—to turn the potential into the actual, the dream into reality. But we can do that only if we are prepared to spend ourselves.

Onions or Daffodils | 101

TWO PEOPLE I KNOW WELL HAD A DEAR FRIEND who died suddenly and prematurely, leaving them in deep grief for many months. They went to her grave in the autumn and planted daffodil bulbs for her. As they planted, they were also planting their sorrow and their loss.

The following spring they returned to the graveside, full of hope that their grief would have turned into bright blossoms. But when they arrived, they found no daffodils dancing in the April breeze. Instead they found a clump of sturdy onion plants! They stood there at their friend's grave and howled with laughter.

Maybe they recalled another of God's promises: "I will turn their mourning into joy. I will console and gladden them after their sorrows" (Jeremiah 31:13). They remember that, amid their own peals of laughter, they distinctly heard their friend laughing along with them.

The dark holds treasures beyond our imagination, and the poverty of a wintering earth contains secret riches, but they reveal themselves in God's time and

God's way. To be a believer is to trust in this unseen becoming.

Only the springtime will reveal whether God is growing my own concerns into daffodils or onions. Either way, today's tears will become tomorrow's laughter.

Theological Exchange | 102

THERE WAS ONCE AN EMINENT HEART SURGEON who liked to debate with his faithful gardener about the existence of God. One day he thought he had clinched the matter: "I have cut open thousands of human hearts," he said, "but I have never seen a soul inside them."

But the gardener had the last word: "I have accidentally sliced through thousands of daffodil bulbs with my spade, through the years, and I have never seen a daffodil inside them."

103 | The Cholera Fountain

One feature in the heart of the city of Dresden, in the former East Germany, is generally missed by the tourists. It never shows up on postcards. It is a beautifully and intricately carved stone water fountain, called the Cholera Fountain, and it dates back to 1845.

At that time the fountain was built for the people of Dresden as an expression of thanksgiving that they had been spared the worst ravages of a cholera epidemic.

The fountain is engraved with some words from Psalm 91:

"You need not fear the terrors of the night,
The arrow that flies in the daytime,
The plague that stalks in the darkness,
The scourge that wreaks havoc at high noon.
Though a thousand fall at your side
Ten thousand at your right hand,
You yourself will remain unscathed."

Almost exactly one hundred years later, in February 1945, a different kind of terror overtook Dresden by night, as allied troops carpet bombed the city from the air. It was well known at the time that Dresden was filled with helpless refugees fleeing the horrors of the Soviet invasion from the east. A different kind of scourge wrought havoc by day, as those who had sought shelter under the bridges over the River Elbe were picked off by machine-gun fire from low-flying aircraft.

The center of Dresden was completely wiped out, and thousands of innocent people died horrible deaths. Only one thing survived intact: the Cholera Fountain.

When my very minor terrors and scourges afflict me, I remember the Cholera Fountain. Not for some promise that the worst thing I fear won't happen to me. Quite the opposite. The Cholera Fountain tells me that the things I most fear may indeed happen, but that they will have no power to extinguish the essential spirit of who I am. Like that flow of pure water from the fountain, the divine life that wells up in every human heart can never be extinguished.

104 | Creative Fire

BUSH FIRES HAVE RAGED THROUGH THESE REGIONS of Australia, the flames devastating everything in their path. Acre upon acre of soaring eucalyptus have been reduced to smoldering ashes. Kangaroos and koalas have fled, or perished. All life has receded.

Next year, however, these plains will be sprouting green again.

The heat that reduces them to cinders is the only heat strong enough to burst open the eucalyptus seeds. If there were no fire, there would be no eucalyptus here.

I remember my mother's cremation: the low, grinding pain in my heart as the curtains closed on her coffin, and she—the dear one who had given me life and taught me how to live it—was consigned to the heat of the fire.

But I think now of the eucalyptus seed. And my heart finds a little ledge of peace to cling to, and my tears make a little waterfall, to give life to tiny seeds, and to something new.

NORTHWEST

Loving with God's Love

We can't love with God's love! Of course we can't. If we could, this world would be something else entirely. But from time to time little shafts of a great light strike through the general mess of daily life, and we know that we are seeing glimpses of a universe that actually runs on love, and means us well. We are seeing strands of a God-presence running right through the fabric of human life.

We see these strands often in the most unexpected people and places and situations. Usually the people who reveal them are completely unconscious of their own transparency to God's light. They are not trying to be special but are simply being who they are.

I invite you to turn beyond the sunset now, and peer into the twilight. You may see some of their silhouettes there, etched against the sky. And they may see yours.

105 | Miss Woodland

THE STRICTEST TEACHER I EVER HAD IS ALSO THE one I recall as the gentlest. For most of the time she taught us mathematics, and she tolerated no nonsense, no lapses of concentration, and no bungled homework. She looked the part: severe, almost to the point of ferocity, with her silver hair impeccably pinned back. But she had another side. Her second passion was the garden. Occasionally she would walk into class with shining eyes and an expression that could only be called a look of love. "Have you seen the snowdrops peeping through, down in the spring gardens?" she would ask us, as if with God's own voice, coaxing the thoughtless to stop and wonder.

We would encourage her of course. Every minute spent with the snowdrops was a minute less of mathematics. We might exchange conspiratorial smiles, but we would nevertheless find a moment to go down to the spring gardens and check out the snowdrops.

She was called Miss Woodland. She was a perfect blend of left-brain logic and right-brain intuition, of discipline and joy. She taught us that the elegance of a perfectly balanced equation and the beauty of a wild flower are just two of the countless faces of the same awesome universe. She died before we left school, and there wasn't a pupil who didn't mourn her passing.

106 | A Father's Love

I DLY I WATCH FROM MY WINDOW AS A YOUNG DAD walks past outside with his small daughter, who is riding her little tricycle and is full of the joys of spring. Then suddenly, out of the blue, she collides with the curb and falls off her bike.

As she bursts into hysterical tears and screams, Dad leaps into action. He pushes aside the overturned tricycle and gathers the little one into his arms, checking for injuries and offering comfort. She continues to scream for a few minutes—this isn't going to be a quick fix. But next time I glance at them, Dad is gently encouraging her to try the bike again. Between subdued sobs, she gingerly begins to pedal again, and they are off, Dad carefully shielding her from the hazardous curb side.

How vividly this reflects incidents when life has jolted me suddenly into a state of shock, and I have screamed at God inwardly in protest at the pain and helpless frustration of it all. But there were never any divine reproaches for not paying sufficient attention. No rebukes, just a gathering into a heart that knows much better than mine that all shall be well, and that the journey must continue.

107 | Searching Questions

A Mennonite woman is asked by a curious observer, "Are you actually a Christian?"

She replies, "Ask my neighbor."

At a Quaker meeting, a visitor breaks the silence to ask the person in the next seat, "When does the service begin?"

The reply: "When the worship is over."

Real Estate | 108

THE BRIGHT YELLOW MALE WEAVERBIRD DOESN'T just build A nest. He builds a veritable hanging basket—a magnificent creation—in the hope of pleasing his desired mate. She watches the proceedings from a nearby vantage point. When he has finished she comes to inspect. He waits, on tenterhooks. You can almost see his little body quivering with nervous anticipation.

Quite probably she will reject his offering. If she does he will start again and try to woo her with a second home, and a third if need be, and a fourth. Some experts say that the male weaverbird will sometimes make up to forty such nests, desperately seeking the approval of the female.

It reminds me of how desperately we sometimes try to please God, fully, but misguidedly, expecting rejection. (Who has taught us that expectation, I wonder?)

But maybe it's the other way around. Maybe God is continually creating a home for us, in this beautiful ever-changing planet, and in the creatures, human and non-human, who enrich our lives. And it is we, not God, who are never satisfied, and keep on insisting on something bigger and better.

The weaverbird will probably give up after forty attempts to please. It's a good thing for us that God is God and not a weaverbird!

Queen of the World | 109

THE REGINA MUNDI CHURCH IN SOWETO, ON THE edge of Johannesburg, was a center of protest gathering during the years of apartheid in South Africa, and subject to brutal police raids. The bullet holes and battered fabric testify to these facts.

This church is certainly a symbol of the struggle and a victim of it. But it is also the site of several of the Truth and Reconciliation Commission hearings that followed.

This church is for real. Forget the palaces of Rome and the baroque splendors of many European churches. This is the real thing! It is akin to the churches of the former East Germany, where the seeds of protest against a domination system grew into radical nonviolent transformation. This church incarnates the gospel.

Regina Mundi, queen of the world, says a costly "No!" to the world's power mongers and a decisive "Yes!" to the reign of God.

110 | Thursday Prayer

My African friend takes me to her home in a black township in South Africa. We wait for her mother to come home. My friend explains that today, being Thursday, is the day the women of the township go to prayer.

What this actually means is that they spend a large part of the day visiting those who are sick, or who have recently been bereaved, or are in some other kind of trouble.

Contemplation in action!

This practice of Thursday prayer is widespread among black women in South Africa, and goes back to the time when domestic servants traditionally had Thursday off, and they spent it in prayer.

How different things might be, if we all turned our prayer into practical action, and if we realized that all our practical action needs to be rooted in prayer. How different things might be if Sunday and Thursday always went hand in hand.

Wee Billy Wilkie | 111

THE CHURCH IS AT THE BOTTOM END OF A SPRAWLING Scottish town. Its drop-in center is open all hours. Liz is on late duty.

Wee Billy Wilkie shuffles in, the worse for drink and barely able to totter on sore, ulcerated feet. Willy is a frequent—and welcome—guest here. Liz knows him, and so, of course, do the local police and townsfolk. They hold him in affection. No one would harm him.

Liz was once a nurse. Tending an ulcerated foot comes naturally, though it's less easy to handle the stench when Billy's battered shoe is removed.

She bathes the foot, gently. Billy relaxes. When she is finished, he stretches out his hand and places it lightly on her shoulder.

"Thanks, Liz. That feels so good."

She looks into his sad, world-wearied eyes. Her own eyes fill with tears. She knows she is gazing into the face of Christ.

112 | No Room at the Inn

A story is told of a children's nativity play. The teacher has rehearsed the scenes thoroughly over the weeks leading up to Advent, and on the big night the parents assemble in the school hall in proud anticipation as their small angels and shepherds take the stage. Then the diminutive Mary and Joseph step into the limelight and knock at the door of the inn. It is then that the six-year-old innkeeper changes the script.

"Please can we have a room for the night," they ask him.

"Sorry there is no room in the inn," he says, according to script.

But at that point the little innkeeper has second thoughts of his own.

"Hang on," he adds. "Don't go away. You can have *my* room."

Can he have *my* room, in all its chaos and confusion? Can he have *yours*?

Wild Child | 113

A slender figure catches my eye down in the underpass. I look more closely and recognize her. She is in the same grade as my daughter. She has a bad reputation; I wouldn't feel too comfortable if my daughter brought her home. She is considered to be a troublesome teenager who flaunts the rules, neglects her schoolwork, and may even be running wild in other respects.

And here she is, with her provocatively short skirt and a defiant expression on her face. She walks through the underpass and makes a beeline for a homeless man sitting down there with his begging bowl. He greets her with a familiar smile; it's obvious that this isn't their first meeting. She squats down beside him for a few minutes' chat and then takes off to the nearby store and comes back with a burger and coke which she sets down beside him, and then sits and keeps him company while he eats.

I can't help watching this scene unfold. I can't help hearing echoes of Jesus' words: "There were once two brothers. The father asked each of them to do something for him. One said of course he would do it. He was always the obedient one. But he never got round to it. The other said 'Give me a break. No time. Things to do, people to see, far too busy.' He was always the difficult one. Then he went away and thought about it, and quietly did what his father had asked. Which of them do you think was closer to the father's love?"

Wild child, how come you are so intimate with God's love and don't even know it, and we who seek it so often miss it?

Transformed by Trust | 114

It's the night of the school Christmas concert. Right in front of me sits a little boy—someone's little brother, who probably should have been in bed at this hour—and his parents. He shuffles and fidgets interminably, continually pushing back his seat to crunch into my knees. I am getting really impatient with him. He (or rather my impatience) is distracting me from the concert and making me feel cross.

Then, in the way children sometimes do, he suddenly gives up the unequal struggle to stay awake, leans his head back on my long-suffering knees, and falls asleep.

Something flips inside me. My impatience melts into something closer to a sense of wonder. My maternal instincts are activated. I contemplate the small tousled head resting so trustfully on my lap. How amazing, that this little stranger should entrust himself, in sleep, to me.

I stop resenting him. I start loving him. I even get a glimpse of how God might see him.

115 | Rule Breaker

MAX WAS A VERY ORDINARY MAN LIVING IN THE former East Germany. He had been a soldier in the First World War. When the Second World War broke out he was working as a foreman in a factory. The factory used Russian girls forcibly taken from their homes to work as slave labor in the German Reich.

Max was uneasy about this. He could see that some of the girls were sick, and all were malnourished. He surreptitiously arranged for the sick girls to have a place to rest, safe from the scrutiny of the Nazi overseers. He showed them all where they could secretly cook themselves some warm soup using the factory's resources.

At home Max erected a false wall in his apartment, to conceal Jews trying to flee from the Holocaust. On Sundays Max always went to church, but he sat alone on the back row. Divorced after a failed teenage marriage, and now remarried, he was excluded from communion.

"Not him," they said. "He broke the rules."

Max's attitude was, "In every situation, stay human." It could have cost him his life. In fact it saved many other lives.

When the Soviet troops stormed Berlin at the end of the war, the German factory managers were all marched away to face exile or imprisonment in a foreign land. When Max was marched out, the girls intervened and spoke up for him.

"Not him," they said. "He was good to us."

The simple humanity of Max softened the hearts of his former enemies.

And yet he lived and died excluded from the sacraments of the church.

116 | Unlikely Friendships

YOU REALLY WOULDN'T WANT TO RUN INTO A BUFFALO on a dark night. They weigh in excess of 2,000 pounds, and their intimidating appearance, complete with horns, doesn't immediately suggest a warm welcome. But they have a friend, a tiny colorful bird called the oxpecker, who thinks nothing of landing on their backs for a meal of ticks, flies and maggots, and bringing its host welcome relief from these parasites.

And you wouldn't want to tangle with a crocodile if you value your life. But another bird, a little plover in East Africa, actually *enjoys* sitting among the crocodile's teeth! It lives on the parasites there, and the crocodile gets a visit to the dental hygienist for free.

These are symbiotic relationships—relationships between unlikely companions, each of whom benefits from the encounter. They have something to teach us. When we live and work for the welfare of one another, a whole new range of possibility opens up and natural fears and enmities can be dissolved.

If We'd Known It Was You . . .

117

A TRAVELING SALESMAN CALLED TODAY. HE WAS only trying TO make a living and he told me about his family. I told him I didn't need anything. If I'd known it was you, Lord, I'd have invited him in.

A neighbor phoned last night. Her baby wouldn't stop screaming and she was at her wits' end. I was just going out and I was running late. If I'd known it was you, Lord, I'd have changed my plans and gone over to give her a little break.

We didn't know it was you, Lord . . .

We didn't see you in the stricken faces of the illegal immigrants being threatened by a crowd of protesters outside the town hall.

We didn't see you in the child being bullied in the schoolyard.

We didn't see you in the difficult patient on the ward, the colleague who wouldn't see things our way, the partner who needed some sympathy when we were busy with our own concerns.

We didn't recognize your face in those who are so different, because we expected you to look just like us!

The Cost of Little Things | 118

A FRIEND WHO IS A DISTRICT NURSE TELLS ME OF her heartache when visiting elderly infirm people. All too often, they live alone, and the visit of a nurse is their only chance to speak to another human being from one week to the next.

Sometimes just some small change would make a big difference to their quality of life. A few hours' help with cleaning. A couple of nails to secure the edge of a carpet and help prevent another fall. A bunch of flowers or a telephone call to brighten a drab existence.

These small things are worth more than a hundred acts of parliament. They cost almost nothing, and yet they cost too much, because they cost love and commitment. The life you have once touched with love, another's need that you have once acknowledged and attended to, becomes a personal responsibility. It's much easier, after all, to leave matters to "the authorities."

119 | Apple Peel

When we eat an apple, we would never simply eat the peel and throw the fruit away. Imagine, all that succulent fruit and the core with its cargo of new apple trees in the form of the seeds it contains. It would be ludicrous to eat only the peel and disregard the rest of the apple.

Yet so many people do exactly that when they are reading or hearing a story, and especially the stories in Scripture. They consume the literal layer of the story and throw the rest away. They ask, "Did this really happen, and if so, when and where and how?" But the real questions are hidden further down: "What does this story mean, and how does it impact the way I am living my life today?"

Think of all that is cast aside with the discarded fruit: the actual substance of the story, the core of meaning, the seeds of potential transformation.

We can have different opinions about the value of eating the peel. Some people always do. Some never do. Some are selective about which peel they eat. Stories are like that. Some are clearly literally true as well as being deeply meaningful. Some are not intended as vehicles of fact, but as carriers of possibility. We can say about many stories: "This story is true, and it may have happened." Whether it actually happened is far less important than the deep truth it contains.

Maybe our preferences about the apple peel don't matter so much. What matters is whether we are willing to take into ourselves the deep truths that lie *beneath* the peel. If our desire is to live and love in the pattern that God reveals through Jesus of Nazareth, then we are going to need the whole apple, and not just the peel.

120 | The Glass Harp

A STREET MUSICIAN IS ENTERTAINING THE CROWDS. I stop TO listen. He plays his tunes on a series of drinking glasses. Some are large, some small, some middle-sized. No two of them are the same. Some are full of water, some are empty, most contain varying amounts of liquid. The result is that every glass creates a different musical note when he taps it with his little baton.

As I watch, I can see us all, the large and the small, the full and the empty, and all the multitude of partway-in-betweens. Each of us is a note in life's ongoing musical. Each of us is indispensable to the symphony that God is composing on planet earth.

There is no audition needed. You simply have to be who you are, small, large, or middling, full, empty, or not quite sure. God will make the music.

NORTH

Destiny

WE HAVE TRAVELED FULL CIRCLE AND FIND ourselves back where we began, facing due North.

Yet we are not the same travelers who first set out from that starting point.

Every step of the journey has been shaping us into who we are today, and today *truly is* the first day of the rest of our lives.

In every direction we have found little shafts of eternal light that transform stones into diamonds. When we thought we were walking through a shower, we caught sight of a rainbow.

When we stubbed our toe on a rock, it surprised us by becoming a stepping stone.

When we felt we were trudging through a barren desert, small gleams of glory sparkled through the pointlessness and gave it meaning.

When we thought the darkness was absolute, we noticed a midnight star.

In the ground of our being the heart's restless compass comes to rest.

Yet there is always a divine "more," urging us forward, and the "more" will take us beyond anything we can ask or imagine.

Memory Keeping | 121

I lived in Berlin for several years during the Cold War. Back then, in the Sixties, West Berlin was an island in the middle of East Germany. It was cold rather than "cool," a half-abandoned city, a city under siege, where people lived under the shadow of division, half expecting a Soviet offensive any day. Above all, it was a city with sinister empty spaces that once had been traversed by life's busy traffic and was now crossed only by barbed wire and a concrete wall.

But this is a return visit, a bit of a nostalgia trip. I take the U-bahn to Potsdamer Platz, which has become arguably the most spectacular example of the city's resurrection. When I lived there, Potsdamer Platz was grim and derelict, bisected by the Berlin Wall, a no-man's land, silent and surreal. Now it throbs with life, its high-rise towers soaring above the milling multitudes, proclaiming "we are risen!"

Two schoolgirl researchers approach me. They ask why I have come to Potsdamer Platz today. "Memories," I say, and describe to them briefly how this part of the city used to be, forty years ago. Then I realize I am telling them about a world of which they have absolutely no inkling—a stark and threatening world, now buried under the dust of time. What for me seems only yesterday is for them distant history. They listen, attentively. But does it matter, whether they hear about it or not?

I think it does, because everything that has happened to and in Berlin—the good, the bad, and the ugly—has made it what it is today, which in turn is the seed of everything it has the potential to become.

What is true for a city is true for every person as well. Our history matters—our collective stories and personal ones. When we listen to our memories, we expose hidden layers of who we are. The memory keepers (all of us) have a sacred duty to share their treasure with those who follow. If we don't, we risk becoming one-dimensional beings with no depth beyond the immediate impulse, no hinterland to lend perspective, and a very diminished sense of who we are.

Let's tell our stories. They are our gift to the future.

Will Tomorrow Ever Come?

122

I PHONE A FRIEND IN AUSTRALIA, HAVING FIRST carefully calculated the time difference, so as not to invade her slumber. We chat for a while, and then I find myself commenting on how good it has been to speak with a human being who has already arrived at "tomorrow." If we should fear for our continuance, I suggest, it would always be possible to speak with an antipodean, and be reassured not only that tomorrow will surely come, but that indeed tomorrow *has* already come. The future lives and breathes, not in some ghostly incorporeal way, but in flesh and blood, mind and spirit.

We laugh at the thought of such reassurance, given to us courtesy of the International Date Line, but underneath the laughter is a different kind of knowledge: Easter knowledge.

What is it that makes us so sure that tomorrow will come—or, rather, that tomorrow is actually already here, a living reality, informing and shaping who we are, and are becoming? My conversation with Australia brings the answer to this question wonderfully into focus. What makes me so sure of tomorrow is that I know someone who is already living it. This isn't someone I have merely heard about or bumped into in catechism or creed. It is someone even more real and present than my friend "down under." I know, with Easter knowledge, the transforming power of his presence because I can see its effects, in myself and in others. I can even speak with him any time in prayer without having to check my watch before I call.

Wisdom's Signature | 123

Sometimes I look into the face of an elderly person and read wisdom's signature there, written in lines and furrows and hollows, and punctuated by the light in his eyes.

And I wonder what story my own face will tell as the years advance, and whether my eyes will shine brightly enough to read it by.

Will I allow my wrinkles and blemishes to trace the story of my experience, and not try to eliminate them? Will I let my eyes disclose my soul's story before they close in death?

124 | The Sound of Silence

A group of teenage boys from an urban high school have been invited to spend a day in the country at a nearby convent.

The elderly sisters are anxious, not without good reason, as the school is notorious for the antisocial behavior of its students.

All through the day they keep an eagle eye out for any signs of trouble, but the boys seem to settle in well enough and respect the prevailing silence and stillness.

At the end of the day—a day blessed with sunshine and blue skies—one of the guests, a burly six-footer, sidles up to the mother superior.

"Can we come again, sister?" he asks, gruffly.

She smiles her assent, and he continues. "I never heard silence before in all my life. And I never heard the birds singing, till today."

Yesterday's Chestnut, Tomorrow's Tree

125

SOMETHING CRUNCHES BENEATH MY FEET. I LOOK down and notice that I'm walking through the broken fragments of last year's chestnut husks.

They look so sad and unremarkable, like the hollowed out cavities of a human life, marking the memories you don't want to remember, the dreams that died at dawn when you woke to the reality of another lonely day.

They remind me of something else too: a cave in a garden in Jerusalem. Above the cave is the inscription: "He isn't here. He is risen."

Could it be that the hollows of our hearts are simply the place where our dreams once lived, and died?

An empty cave warns us not to search for our heart's living dreams in yesterday's graves. They are not there; they are risen. They have grown beyond themselves, and we may not recognize them in their transformed shape, if we are clinging to the idea of how they used to look.

126 | The Other Side of Sorrow

We all hope for happiness. Many would say it is their birthright, to be happy.

Happiness sometimes lies on the roadside of our lives, easily gathered in parcels of pleasure.

But joy is a rarer treasure and often lies only on the other side of sorrow, just as the sweetest fruits often grow on the other side of the thorn hedge.

Maybe happiness can even be a barrier in our search for deeper joy—a seductive cul-de-sac that can tempt us to settle for less, when God longs to give us more.

Who Were We? | 127

CAVE PAINTINGS, PICTOGRAPHS, PETROGLYPHS . . . signs and symbols revealing glimpses of how our early ancestors lived, how they saw themselves and the world around them. Such relics might inspire us to wonder what archaeologists might discover in two thousand years if they excavate our world: computer parts, beer cans, plastic containers, baseball caps?

These might well constitute the detritus of the twenty-first century. But would we want our distant successors to think that's all we were about?

It sets me thinking. If I could leave some "signs and symbols" behind of who I am, who *we* are, what might they be? What might more truly and fully capture a glimpse of what it means to be human on planet earth in our times?

Perhaps, on reflection, what truly defines us is not something we can take hold of, store in a canister, and preserve for posterity. Not an object at all, but a subject. My dream is that future generations might look back on our times and say not so much: "This is what they produced" but "This is how they *were*." And I hope that "how we were" and "who we were" will not feature military conquest or commercial success but those quiet efforts by ordinary people to help us all become more fully human and fully alive: young people who give up years of their lives to serve their brothers and sisters in the developing world; people with the courage to speak their truth in the face of injustice and abuse; people who simply take the time to attend to the silent cries of the people who live next door or work at the next desk.

Who, and how, would we like our great-grandchildren to think we were, when the true history is written? How that true history works out is in our hands. We are creating it.

Einstein for Beginners | 128

A FRIEND WHO RUNS A REHAB CENTER FOR ALCOHOLICS in the inner city shares her wisdom about how to break free of old patterns of mind and life:

"If you always think what you always thought,
you will always do what you always did,
and you will always get what you always got."

Einstein said much the same thing: "You will never solve a problem with the mindset that created it."

Only a new mind and a new heart will move us forward—which, as it turns out, is exactly what God has offered us!

129 | Where Two Roses Meet

ONCE UPON A TIME TWO STEMS GREW FROM A single rose bush. One grew up the side of a garden wall. The other found its way through a chink in the stone and grew up the other side of the wall. Neither knew of the other's existence, though they sprang from a single root.

Eventually, after years had passed, two roses met and intertwined at the top of the wall. They knew each other from somewhere deep in the past, yet took each other completely by surprise at what each had become.

Might our destiny include such meetings and entwinings? Such reconciliations after estrangements, between man and woman, between humankind and the rest of creation, between us and God?

I suspect that all that springs from the single root in the heart of God is destined to meet in a unity that eclipses all differences.

Lamplight, Sunlight | 130

IN MY LITTLE HOUSE THE LAMPS ARE BURNING IN every room. Outside the night is dark; inside it would be just as dark, were it not for these little lamps. They make me feel safe. They give me identity. They are the things I cherish, the things I can't imagine being without: my health and strength, my five senses, my mobility, my intellect, my circle of friends, the security of being accepted by my own tribe, my comfort zones of every kind.

So I live in dread of any of these lamps being extinguished. I cling to them; everything I think I am depends on them.

But then something happens. Outside a new dawn is breaking. Beyond and around and above my house, my safe little box, the sun is rising.

Its dazzling brightness draws me beyond myself, beyond my house. I walk out, in awe and wonder at this greater light and warmth.

The lamps in my house are still burning, but they are barely discernible in the brightness of daybreak. I can't even remember whether I have switched them off. It doesn't matter anymore. The morning eclipses them all. And I choose to set my face toward the new day.

Growing Up

131

When I was a little girl, my mother always seemed to buy me clothes that were too big for me, on the basis that I would soon grow into them.

When my own baby was born, I also bought clothes a few sizes beyond "newborn," because I knew that she would need that size only for a few short weeks.

I'm beginning to understand now that God's Dream for us, and for creation, works on the same principle. The life, the love, and the dreams that come from God are always a few sizes too big for us. We can choose to put them away in a drawer labeled "impossible dreams" or "just idealistic thinking."

Or we can choose to grow into them.

God knows we *can,* just as a mother knows her baby can and will grow into those bigger clothes. And Jesus shows us what it looks like when humanity grows into God's Dream.

132 | The Lilac Tree

I WANDER QUIETLY AROUND THE SMALL, ENCLOSED garden sheltering the inner courtyard of the old abbey. A few wild-looking trees fill up most of the space and spread themselves over the grass and the narrow path. The windows of the chapel glance down, as if to wonder who will ultimately claim this space—the steady age-molded, rain-stained stones or the thrusting and exuberant springtime growth?

I come up against a mass of snarled-up, winding branches that occupy a whole corner of the courtyard. At first I see only the knots and tangles, as the thick arms of bark and branch struggle for primacy.

They remind me of the messes of wool I used to create as a child when my aunt tried to teach me to knit, patiently disentangling my every failure. I relate them to my life's tangles that tighten and toughen, the harder I pull at them.

These branches remind me also of the demoniac who called out of the caves and knew his name was Legion, for there were many of him. I see in them the multiplications of my own compulsions and contradictions.

Yet there is peacefulness in this courtyard. It provides a space in which chaos can be recognized and acknowledged, touched by a healing hand.

I reach out to touch the tangled branches. I feel their roughness, like the coat of a strange, untrustworthy dog who might bite, but, today, allows himself to be approached. I become aware of a steady source of love somewhere beneath my feet, in unseen roots.

Then I'm aware of a fragrance all around me, penetrating my pores and settling into the labyrinth inside. *This is a lilac tree!*

High above me is a trellis of green and clustering white. The blossom draws my focus beyond the suffocating snarls and tangles. I understand that joy is implicit in the fact of pain. Winter branches trust and wait through the ages, for the moment of blossom. The promise of peace that doesn't deny or cancel out the pain, but becomes its ultimate statement.

133 | Stepping Stones

When Indiana Jones comes to the edge of the chasm, he knows that there may or may not be a bridge across it. He will not find out whether the hoped for bridge is really there unless he steps out with one foot and risks the drop.

For me the chasm is the rest of the story . . . my own story and the story of humanity on planet earth. Is there a future? Does the universe mean well toward us? Dare we risk that step of trust into the unknown, unseen, uncharted terrain of all that might be?

I see myself standing on the banks of a fast-flowing river. I know I must cross, but there is no bridge. Then a figure, a Christ-figure, comes to me carrying a large boulder, and places it in front of me, in the river, inviting me to step out onto it. Every day he brings another boulder, another stepping stone. Every day I move farther into the waters, balancing precariously on my fragile faith.

One day he is late. I turn around, mid-river, and only then do I see where the boulders are coming from. He is systematically de-constructing my cozy little cottage on the shore, in order to turn it into stepping stones for my onward journey.

He is using my past to create my future.

He is asking me to reach out with both hands—one to let go of all I thought I couldn't live without, and one to reach toward everything I thought I could never attain.

134 | Reef Encounter

I DROP FROM THE BOAT INTO THE WARM WATERS OF the Great Barrier Reef, equipped with snorkeling gear, and allow the currents to carry me over these blue deeps. Another world opens up below me, a world in which I am a stranger, an alien even, and yet the teeming fish and the gleaming corals don't seem to mind me too much.

Then I find myself floating just a few feet above a magnificent turtle. I hold my breath, for fear of disturbing the holy peace that seems to surround her. She is an ancient traveler, carrying ancestral memories of times when all life was lived in such waters and humankind was but a future dream.

She has made a journey, guided by this deep memory and steered by her awareness of every current, every magnetic field, every subtle change of light and shadow. She has survived in spite of all that has come against her—predators, pollution, and perilous weather systems. Her determination has brought her halfway across the globe, in search of the beach where she was born.

In this silent meeting on the reef, I know that she is part of me, and I am part of her, and that we are both held in the recesses of earth-memory. We travel doggedly toward the place where our sacred source is at one with our divine destiny

135 | Traveling Light

A FRIEND SENDS ME A STORY HE HAS HEARD. AN apprentice long-distance truck driver is about to make his first major journey. He will travel for thousands of miles across Canada. It is late at night as he prepares to set off.

He climbs into the driver's cab and switches on the engine. The headlights come on. He follows the path of light they make and realizes that it reaches only a few hundred yards into the surrounding darkness. He thinks of the thousands of miles that lie ahead. He asks himself, *How could I be so foolish as to set off on a journey of thousands of miles when my lights reach only a few hundred yards?*

Perhaps his fears overwhelm him, and he switches off the engine, climbs out of the cab, and gives up the whole idea.

Or perhaps he starts to move forward. If he does, he will discover that the light travels with him.

Homecoming | 136

THE LITTLE VILLAGE WHERE MY FATHER'S FAMILY has its roots has hardly changed at all. The irrigation channels still flow through these flatlands, brown and slow, alongside the sandy Lincolnshire fields. The hedgerows, where my cousins and I played as children, still stand untroubled by the passage of time, and the village still has fewer than five hundred inhabitants.

It has been nearly three decades since I journeyed back to the lanes and farmsteads and ditches and hedgerows of these left-but-never-forgotten homelands. I used to sleep in a small bedroom tucked into the end gable of my grandmother's cottage in this village, and I could look out of its tiny window, barely a foot square. I used to gaze out of this window for a few minutes every morning when I woke up and every night before I went to bed. Over the years it took on a sacred quality for me, which I recognized only when time and circumstance had distanced me from it.

It was such a very small window and it contained such a very large view. Its compact frame held nothing less than the universe, for my child's vision. A wideness of brown furrows that seemed to be the very highway of my life. A network of irrigating streams. A line of poplars, providing the horizontal axis and drawing my gaze to the distant horizon. In the center of the view was my aunt and uncle's farmstead, standing proud against the sky, braving whatever the heavens might bring, whether threat or promise. And the sun always set behind the farmstead, inviting me to sleep peacefully.

Since those days I have traveled the world and made friends on every continent. Yet I feel a moment's trepidation as I ring the bell of the house that now stands where my grandmother's cottage once stood, and where my remaining relatives still live. Will they even recognize me after all these years? Will they welcome the prodigal cousin who arrives unannounced at their door?

I needn't have worried. The door opens, and my cousin Pat lets out a cry of delighted amazement. "Margaret—what a wonderful surprise! I was thinking about you just this morning." I fall into a loving embrace, and I know I am home. I know it because I can feel the deep sap of life rising up from these roots, through the lives of all my forebears, through my own life, and on into the lives of my daughter and granddaughter.

Perhaps all our lives are like that little window, one foot square, framed by our own "threescore years and ten." Yet the view is immense. It contains all that has made us who we are and reveals the possibility of all we might become. And above all, it welcomes us home with the enduring glow of love.

137 | Closing Down, Opening Up

THE SUNSET IS BREATHTAKINGLY BEAUTIFUL VIEWED from the window of the aircraft, so high above the earth. A gradually deepening band of the rainbow spectrum encircles the earth, folding it into sleep.

I feel a twinge of sadness as I watch the light fade on all that it means to be alive and aware on a living planet. But when the last glow fades into the west, a much vaster landscape will reveal itself: the stars. A range of visibility of a few miles will expand exponentially into light years, billions of light years, spiraling back to the first beginnings of what we call our universe.

Surely, after all, there is no dying. Like the sunset, what seems like a closing down is in truth an opening of unimaginable proportions.

Acknowledgments

THIS BOOK HAS TWO GODPARENTS, AND THOUGH I have given birth to it, its gestation owes a great deal to these two people. I thank Joe Durepos of Loyola Press, who first raised the idea with me, and encouraged me to run with it. Joe is a never-failing goldmine of inspiration, wisdom, and encouragement, and I am deeply grateful to him. At the other end of the pregnancy, I thank Vinita Hampton Wright, who is the book's midwife. I thank Vinita not only for her sensitive editing, but for who she is, for her wisdom, her gentle strength, her hospitable heart, and her enquiring mind. Joe and Vinita are part of a great team at Loyola Press, many of whom I have had the pleasure of meeting personally. So I thank all of you, headed by Terry Locke, for welcoming me into your Chicago-kingdom and making me feel at home not just in the Windy City but in your offices, where another wind, the wind of the Spirit, blows.

The reflections in the book owe their existence to a thousand different people, many of whom I will never know by name. People who passed me in the street, people who said or did something inspirational or thought-provoking, people who sat with me in the dark and danced with me in the joyful times, people who reminded me that we are all fragments of a vast and breathtaking story. All of us are only who we are in relation to everyone else, and every passing encounter is shaping our own unique identity. The book reflects just a few of those life-giving encounters.

Some of the reflections first appeared in *America* magazine and I am very grateful to its editors for inviting me to be a columnist and for giving permission to adapt and reproduce some of this material in book form.

Almost everything I write, and especially this book, owes more than I can ever repay to Ignatius Loyola, and to his spiritual sons and daughters in our own times, my Jesuit friends and mentors, and the many sisters and laypeople who also follow the Ignatian way. Very especially I thank Gerard Hughes SJ and Brian McClorry SJ who have long been, and I hope will always remain, dear friends and wise guides who first introduced me to the riches of Ignatian spirituality and continue to accompany my explorations.

Finally I would like to thank the people in the small faith-sharing group that has become my spiritual home and anchor point. Thank you Jane and Bernard, Eunyce and Colin, John, Chris and Rowena. You have nourished and sustained me more than you will ever know.